THE SMALL BUSINESS STARTER'S GUIDE
Sharing 30 Years' Experience on How to Build for Success

Also by 'Muyiwa Osifuye

FAST TRACK YOUR BUSINESS
-18 Steps On Ideas, Marketing, Self And Employee Management-

THE SMALL BUSINESS STARTER'S GUIDE

Sharing 30 Years' Experience on How to Build for Success

'MUYIWA OSIFUYE

To

my eternal Muse,
as always – perpetual gratitude.

and

O, S & T
- the trio

Copyright © 2016 by 'Muyiwa Osifuye

All rights reserved. No portion of this book may be reproduced – mechanically, electronically, or by any other means, including photocopying – without written permission of the publisher.

ISBN-13:978-1535554466
ISBN-10:1535554460

Contact:
mosifuye@gmail.com
contact@muyiwaosifuye.com

Stom and Ruby Services, Lagos, Nigeria
(small business consulting)
www.muyiwaosifuye.com

Contents

INTRODUCTION

CHAPTER 1
Your Mindset & The World Of Business ... 1

CHAPTER 2
The Marketing Plan ... 19
How To Make A Million In Sales ▫ Where To Get Your Customers?

CHAPTER 3
The Organizational Plan ... 28
Organizational Structure ▫ Legal And Regulatory Requirements ▫ Types Of Business Formations ▫ Naming The Business ▫ The Underground Kingpins ▫ Building For Performance ▫ The Organogram And Relationships ▫ Creating A System ▫ Managing Employees ▫ Measuring Activities For Profitability ▫ Profitable Business Models ▫ Beauty Of Equipment Leasing ▫ Your Network As Asset Gains ▫ Gains In Value Chain ▫ Why Not Produce The Input? ▫ Retailing Your Production ▫ How Entrepreneurs Reduce Risks? ▫ Growth As Mixed Blessings ▫ Multiplying The Business

CHAPTER 4
The Financial Planning ... 64
What Will Save Your Business? ▫ The Reality Of Franchise ▫ Working Capital ▫ Your Industry's Admission Score ▫ Home-Based And Alternatives ▫ Acquiring Your Tools ▫ Financing Without Money ▫ The Business Plan Mystery ▫ Pains Of Financing ▫ Cash-flow: The Life Line ▫ Expenses Aren't The Same ▫ Different Shades Of Profit ▫ Be Smart; Keep The Records ▫ Take Cash, Not Profit ▫ Surviving Recession ▫ Other Side-Incomes ▫ How To Tame Business Risks? ▫ Crowding To Fund ▫ Twists About M & A

CHAPTER 5
Technology For Business ... 103
Technology And Vigilance ▫ Filtering Information Overload ▫ Website As Capital Asset ▫ The Easy Way To Grow

CHAPTER 6
Your Daily Activities ... 115
Developing An Effective Routine

CHAPTER 7
Your Success & Mistakes ... 119

CHAPTER 8
Appraisals & The Score Sheet ... 121

CHAPTER 9
Is Your CSR Missing The Target? ... 123

CHAPTER 10
What Is Next? ... 128

Free Resources & Other Books ... 130

About The Author ... 131

Introduction

This business book is my concise account of over 30 years in the rough, exciting but rewarding journey of entrepreneurship, in servitude and as a business owner...

Before I go straight into the essence of this book for start-ups and business owners, I need to share a few thoughts about the disruption going on in the world of business today.
Every small business owner must reflect on these observations to be assured of progress and understanding. For the fact that a business does not exist in isolation. Businesses and fortunes have been greatly affected. It is not only the so-called technology that has created disruption in the world of commerce.
There are others. They affect business. They affect our fortune. They affect individuals. They affect countries and they affect many other things, directly or indirectly.

Terrorism and failed governance are disruptive. The attendant forced immigration in our world today has created a seismic shift in politics and commerce in many parts of the world.
Majority of businessmen and women were not ready for these.
Fortunes have been threatened to a large extent.

New entrepreneurial opportunities thankfully, have become the lot of some idle hands.
These are creative minds that could solve these myriad of problems as a result of this unwelcome development.
Old economic blocs are at the verge of complete disintegration - with threats and opportunities for businesses. Small business owners are affected by the ripple effect.
If you are reading this as one, think about it. It is real.
Your decisions into the future will be affected. Humans are the ones making these things happen as usual.

No entrepreneur can be boastful of what tomorrow will throw up. But we can try to conjecture. So to go into business is all about risk. But many make success of it while the majority do not!
It is a mishmash of different strokes of sorts.

However discerning an enterprise owner could be, he or she must really look and join the dots as events unfold. To come up with a hazy picture for the future which could become our reality?
That one we will touch, feel and experience in the real sense of it, eventually. That is the space which enterprise owners and other players have found themselves. Yet we must operate as business owners in our delicate world...

ℜ ℜ ℜ

Having cleared that away from my mind, let us proceed with this book of business empowerment, which is seemingly lean but embedded with sieved out practical basics for business start-ups.

Thoughts shared here are the fundamentals, whether it is a home-based, out of home, physical business or online business, it does not really matter; the foundation must be understood.
Business is about relating with our world as a platform while we interact with other people as producers of items of values which could be physical or intangible.

The experience garnered in spite of my MBA way back in 1991 can only complement the other hard earned practical lessons. The latter garnered from being rubbed in the mud of enterprise management while you are expected to come out smelling like a freshly cut bunch of roses.
That is the reality of being in business.

This is not to put fear into you as my reader but to prepare your mind to the reality of being a business owner.
It goes beyond the pristine classroom setting of the business school or theories from Professors who have never sold lemonade. However we need all lessons across the spectrum- classroom and outside of it.

Who is this start-up manual for?

It is for a small, maybe, a medium business owner who needs the basics of starting and managing an on-going business. That individual who desires to be led by the hand to be empowered with essentials needed towards a successful enterprise.

Many small businesses fail quickly for many reasons at the early stages. However discouraging the statistics, you can learn from me, here, how to avoid these experiences.

However, as much as possible, this is book moves away from too much an academic slant, for ease of assimilation.
The thoughts shared here will nurture your mind about practical choices to make. The book may also reveal where you possibly went wrong in taking some actions. You will discover a need for a different outlook in becoming a successful entrepreneur.
Would you say this book is about business coaching? The answer is partly, Yes and No! You would have come to your own conclusion, going through my thoughts in this small business book.

So, how do you go from here? You need a workable and intelligent order of activities that must be deployed.
This is what I personally thought through after all these years and I concluded on the **M.O.F.T**. sequence. *There will be exceptions as in all rules.*

When you contemplate starting a business, start thinking in this order:

The **M**arketing Plan,

The **O**rganizational Plan,

Financial Planning and

Technology for Business

This order makes up part of the battle plan. This order of actions will be explained further in the subsequent chapters. But first let us talk about you. You are the business owner or founder, right? Do you have the guts?
Lets see...

1
Your Mindset & The World Of Business

Before you jump-ship into any business or if you are already into one, this is the time to reflect and do a critical self-audit or self-appraisal. Your running a business must equally give you eternal joy, rather than it flogging your soul. It should be a part of your existence. It is either you cherish doing it or you look elsewhere.

And **nobody** must truncate that need for self-preservation and survival, as long as you pursue that dream, within the ethics and having respect for others.
You use your enterprise you have been nurturing as a vehicle for survival and to attain other lofty ideals, otherwise seek being employed in a company where you await a salary or a pay.

Your business goals must be spelt out. It must be measurable. It must be time bound, with clear milestones. Your business must evolve and not be static. It must be valuable to the market place. And above all, the experience must be pleasing to your soul, your customers and contributory in a positive way to our common humanity.
That is tough, right? But, take the assurance that many are presently meeting these goals despite the huge challenges.

Before you go fully into business, it is advisable that you have worked under somebody before. But that may not apply to you if you are courageous enough to learn the ropes as you trudge on. That means you have factored the risks of this uncertainty into your life, as you take the plunge. Better still, get a mentor or a consultant! That's being smart!

At the time I was an employee, my former employers made good decisions and they also erred. I saw them all. From the side-line, I garnered free knowledge from these experiences. As an entrepreneur myself, I have experienced my own fair share of successes and failures.

°MUYIWA OSIFUYE

But don't let us glamorize failure as some business gurus would like you to do.
Don't. It is painful. I have experienced it.

You should not be persuaded to become a self-employed person. The conviction has to come from within. This is what gives you the emotional strength, to wade through the challenges of running an enterprise and the confidence to enjoy the fruits of your labour.

In this our present world of oppression and inequality, there are more opportunities in leveraging your financial status, through entrepreneurship. I will show much later how to do that in this business start-up blueprint.

Therefore, do not go into business with just a mere flash of emotion. You must think it through. Ensure you have put aside a financial backup to take you for at least nine months. To be candid with you, I didn't have much when I started in 1986 - as a side attraction - and again fully in 1994.

If you are in employment, be convinced that the idea has been practically tested by you before you resign. Half a loaf is better than nothing; in case things don't go as planned. Profits may not come as envisaged.

An overhyped business plan - by the most expensive consulting firm in the world - may not prepare you for the unexpected problems of our world. Do a simple business plan if you choose to have one but open all your senses to all stimuli around you, and always.

Talk less and soak in more; you gain free insights by so doing. I was a victim of not being a good listener – though not any longer. When you talk, let it be more of questions. This keeps you to be better informed, as always, than suffocating people with too much of your sermon.

I am aware some people just find themselves in the sudden cold world of unemployment. They have been laid off from work or for some other reasons. That is understandable...
But you will have to patch through, before you can raise your head above the waters.
Otherwise, be cautious of your emotional overconfidence and overstretched self-pity before you set out.
Your spouse may or may not help matters at the critical state of making these important decisions. Listen to your inner soul and if possible seek an honest mentor who is experienced in business or get a consultant. Before you initiate anything, I will repeat, as much as you can, strive to put enough money aside for you and your family. If you are favoured to have the support of your spouse, to handle this aspect; good for you to take the plunge.

But if anything goes awry, due to delayed profits, be sure you can handle the expected nagging from your partner. If you are not sure of support and you do not have some savings already set aside, do not depend on your partner. Wait for the time when you have adequate resources.

So you want to start a business into self-employment...right?

Ok, then. Lets go.

You will have lurking behind your consciousness, how to resolve personal, family and social matters. All these fight for your attention as you attend to the business, whether it is home-based or located elsewhere. You must handle these matters carefully in other not to lose the needed focus.

°MUYIWA OSIFUYE

Let me open your eyes into what it takes, in terms of the personality disposition that is needed, as you consider this path in your life.

You will be told that the path of entrepreneurship is likely to get you to be financially independent. And again it is expected this will give you the power to making your own decisions about your life.

I am assuming, you probably haven't heard what I am about to tell you as you prepare on this interesting journey.

You may have your reasons for the fact that, you have suddenly found yourself being unemployed?

You aspire to be like the successful founders of enterprises you see around or hear about?

Could it be due to loss of your job?
Or you have suddenly come into money, wishing to make good returns on your investments? That is, being in control of your seed capital?

It is even possible you have discovered some ideas, in your mind, that you are convinced or feel the whole world would latch onto and thereafter you would get paid handsomely for these ideas?
You are already salivating and dreaming of your affluence, isn't it?

You may even be tired of the fact that you have been under-employed and under-paid. And maybe, jobs don't stick with you for long or vice versa.
Now, this is what I want you to know, right away.

And that is, your own inherent self-appraisal must first be sorted out. This is the gym training of both your physical and mental muscles that must be ready to go the whole hog of entrepreneurship.

We are simply talking in other words about your mindset!

Some of these qualities you probably have them, but I will assume you are not aware of how important they are.
And I will mention and describe them for you to know, as they are needed to save your life, reduce your frustration and anxiety.

These nagging issues do come up for business owners. Therefore, you need to develop a particular mindset like most serious entrepreneurs. This is to ensure your business goals are attained and while your essence as a person will still be intact.

The growing business is never a straightforward graph.
Not at all.
It has its twists, turns, bends and curves. But you should be prepared to steer the bobbing ship of your enterprise through turbulence and also welcome favourable winds at sea.
There is no excuse, for you as an entrepreneur.

As a founder or chairman of an enterprise, your circumstance is a bit different from a CEO who suddenly is invited to take over an existing company. This is irrespective if such a company is in a position of crises or stability.

As a starter you must have a stable frame of mind, to put up structures and all the basic resources in place. It does not matter whether you have access to free funds or not. Though, having easy money may make things much easier, giving you less mental stress, but if it's not well managed, your creativity could be killed.

At the initial stage of starting, you probably must believe in yourself, that you will have to burn the bridges behind you and therefore there is no going back. You must develop the mental strength likened to that of a stubborn goat. You know goats are stubborn!

°MUYIWA OSIFUYE

You must be assertive and not necessarily proud because the latter can prevent help from where you least expect.

Your multiple academic qualifications should not be a hindrance but you must also develop an all-embracing personality.

The initial phase of the business will make you feel like an errand boy. So be ready to accept to be rubbed in the mud, even from those you feel are below you.

You must learn how to reach out to the public. Let me quickly say, that you are not alone, amongst most entrepreneurs. People will knock off some of your pride. Be ready to live a lonely life before the business really breaks forth from its infancy.

When it is thriving, this is when people will come around you like bees, which they are. You and your business collectively is the sweet nectar. You were being watched all the while during your months and years of dripping sweat and daily grind.

Friends will come forward with business ideas; craftily learn to say, "No" before, "Yes". Follow your instincts because victory could be intoxicating and you may become vulnerable.

Detractors in your industry and government agencies will definitely show up to push you around. Run the business within the laws of the land. Handle them with wisdom and boldness. When you can afford it eventually, get a good but considerate lawyer in your arsenal of running the business. But be careful of lawyers! A personal experience taught me the hard way. I had to let go of a case, I could have pushed to win.

Far-flung family relations praising your expertise and smartness and of course, the bankers - you were chasing earlier on - will beg you to take their loans.

All these categories of people you cannot run away from; handle them to the best of your capability. Whatever business ideas that are brought to you, find ways on your own - quietly - to find out if they will be rewarding. Listen to your instinct before investing in such.
Most times, these ideas are not worth it. It is not their money and resources at risk. Follow you path and be focused. Kill the greed inside of you.

If you choose to invest in another person's upstart, do your proper background check and be knowledgeable of that industry. Get hold of an expert in the industry to help you out. Thereafter - since your funds are there - endeavour to monitor what goes on in that business.

Also, do not be too greedy by dabbling into too many ventures. You can only monitor a few investments, you know…

And do not, at any point in time, plough all your cash reserve into another investment, no matter how attractive it may look. Minimize your risk by investing only a portion of your savings which would have come from your staggered profits. If the terms are right, consider using additional credit facility, from your bank. Determine that the interest rate charged can be absorbed by the carefully studied returns of the investment. But leave room for disappointments.

Turn detractors to friends and watch them, eternally! In dealing with them, you may have to negotiate with them for your peace of mind. Be connected in the right places. In anticipation of your business present and future needs, pick and nurture relevant relationships. Be deliberate in your choice.

You seek successful entrepreneurs like you; to bond and share notes with. It helps. If you are shy, you can work around it by ultimately doing the network bit by bit. You don't need to be an extrovert but your network must be developed. Get out of your comfort zone and get the dust on your shoes, out there. In due course, you will be awarded your own deserved golden boots.

Service the important relationships, even if you are an introvert. I agree you may not like interacting with other people; your business can still do very well if you can handle human issues very well.
But don't be beggarly in your orientation when networking, you will lose more than you would gain. Therefore seek knowledge about human behaviour, generally. What happens around us may not be readily be obvious until we take the pains to be conscious.

There will be times you will be cold or hot. There will be times you will appear to be timid, other occasions; intimidating. Your purpose is your business goal and personal objectives which must be ethical and fair to all. Never lose your guard to lose your business – *being your vehicle for survival in this world*. Never!

If you get help from genuine close friends, and well informed loved ones and family, you are just one of the few lucky entrepreneurs out there. Don't blame anybody, if they don't understand your pursuit. They won't, especially, at the particular time of onset; some of them may not be emotionally ready to join you in your activities for such *a risky venture of entrepreneurship.*

There will be periods or phases of conquest and celebration. You will know what hard work and whatever bit of luck were responsible in the life cycle of the business. You will develop the mind to be a man or a woman of great faith in yourself and the Great Divine.
I am not preaching or proselytizing any religion here, please.

Your intuition, gut feelings or hunch must be well developed. Research has proven many successful business owners use this as the last resort when faced with a dilemma in decision making. Not all your decisions can be scientifically proven or explainable. Logic fail at times. So develop your inner mind.

This means, you must cultivate the habit common with most successful entrepreneurs. That is, having a scheduled time out for introspection, day dreaming, thinking and meditation. But not to lose sight of the practical realities of our situation and our environment in which we operate and exist.
I perceive *entrepreneurs as somewhat priests of enterprise, of the environment and of our humanity.*

Believe you me; things may go well for you, far beyond your efforts. We strike luck at times. It may be rare but it is a reality. But do not plan your business on luck or wishful thinking. Do the needful - the real work. I do not believe those who feel, there is no luck. Don't listen to them. It is not in all cases that we can defer to the dogma of *"cause and effect"* in our lives and endeavours.

Don't get me wrong, having said so. The same *"cause and effect"* tend to play the most prominent role in our circumstances but there are also unexplainable occurrences - good or bad.

Therefore, you need to work hard towards identifiable goals and results, and if luck or benevolent grace meets your efforts, then that will be an icing on the cake. So go ahead and bake the cake and if the icing comes or not, it does not really matter. You will still have the cake, which matters.

There are advices that will be bandied around in your industry or elsewhere. Take the ones useful for your business. Be ethical and do not allow your demanding situation make you greedy. A little secret is that you can always transfer ideas from a different industry to your business to beat competition.

You and other players in your industry run the business the same way. That is sad. No wonder everybody gets same results. It took me a long time to discover the need to change my business approach; as long as the law is not broken.
Your mind must be dynamic.
Go further and put aside a resource that is expendable and try other uncommon ways of being more productive in your business. If that works, you are seen as a genius and the business is better for your creative innovation.
If it fails, it was worth a try, but you are consoled in that you wisely used just a portion of your resources to test the waters.

Making decisions is about taking risks, which you must. Entrepreneurs take calculated risks having gone through due assessment. With time decision must be made by you on a daily basis. You never know which would be successful despite your prior studies. All efforts are risky.
But seating on the fence too long will not do you any good.

Entrepreneurship throws up a lot of discipline in your personality if you wish to succeed eventually. It has taught me that, I can't just do certain things like some non-business owners; painfully so. This is more relevant until your business has reached a maturity phase where others could be delegated to or take over from you.

I have mentioned to you that, being self-employed is about you and service to the market place. While you are it, you must realize that managing your business should never be seen as an exercise of proving to people; of your ingenuity or superiority.

Please, you are not showing off to anybody. That is a path to personal and business disaster. You are not making a point to anybody. It is an undertaking; to better your lot and the society. It is not a 100 meters race with others. It is a long haul.

Your goals will be different from others, and must be.
Why? Many entrepreneurs have developed anxiety. This has lured a few business owners into permanent depression, bothering on suicidal tendencies.
The secret is to tell yourself; *"I will simply do my best"*.
Be convinced you have done so. And leave the rest.
When things don't go well - after the little cry in your closet -dust yourself up. Ask yourself, if you should pursue same efforts through another approach or look elsewhere.

The point is that, if you are very diligent, you will be rest assured that if things don't go on well, it may not be your fault. It might as well be due to factors beyond your powers.
And if it is due to your own fault, then don't blame yourself too much. Take action and rectify things or start all over again. It is your life.
You came alone and we will all depart the world, alone.

Be wary of information overload, in our world of today. Learn from them, identify a pattern of solutions. Develop a critical thinking mindset. Filter through them and use what's applicable to you, from what you have garnered.
How do you get this done? For me, I have been attracted to a lot of information out there. What I do is to soak them in and find time to conclude on what I think will make my life and business much better from the pieces of information.

I regret taking a wrong advice in the year 2002, when I was a novice in a new venture. My instincts told me the advice was inadequate but since I knew no better, I listened to the "expert" who I thought knew it all. This inadequate piece of advice eventually disrupted my business for some years until I recovered, to discover the truth of how to go about that aspect of my business.

The saving grace I had was that I had already diversified into other businesses at a much earlier time. The person who gave the advice was simply a mentally lazy person, as I discovered during that painful experience. His world view was an impractical picture about the world of enterprise.

On the flip side of the coin, advice could be very beneficial. A former colleague told me about the location of direct suppliers that sold me some goods at a cheaper price. Before now, for over 20 years, I had bought same supplies at a higher price from a middleman who claimed he was a direct supplier.

Find out and educate yourself about your industry and other successful thought leaders. This will broaden your mind. It is imperative to read other people's biography; you will get a snippet of them.

But I learn more from people being interviewed, especially when they are unprepared for it. Interviews are more revealing of the truth than crafted biographies.

Because you need to learn from everywhere and anywhere, this makes you work smarter and more effective. Learning must be forever to succeed as a self-employed.

I just learnt - as I write - how a 14 year old is inching to his first million dollars. He started at 9.

Remember your business, will be very demanding at the initial phase. However, it should be balanced with your life and attention given to loved ones within reasonable means. Truth must be told, you can't have a balanced situation when you are still dealing with the teething problem of a new business. Something, somewhere must reach a compromise with you, at the early stage. That is one of the sacrifices you must be ready to give, to stay focused. You can relax much later with a capable team, to have a more balanced life.

It is important to manage your time, by putting up realistic goals, scheduled across the weeks and months. And of course, a good system of taking care of your business must be developed and entrenched as soon as possible.
A written down statement of how things must be done. This must interrelate within the business and with the outside world. This is the business system that will make the business work into the future, even in your absence.

Watching your health is of paramount importance especially at the initial stage of your business, because in your absence - depending on the makeup of your business - the business might stall. Watch what you eat and not because it is in front of you. You will be very busy and have much to do but keep to an exercise schedule.

There are occasions you know you must get a task done but you don't feel like it. Take a break.
How long; I can't tell you, maybe a few minutes…an hour? But bury your head in that task, once you finish relaxing. You need resilience.

The initial efforts of building your business will increase your stress level over time. Therefore you must find the time, either a day in a week, just to do nothing but sleep and relax with non-work activities.

The body needs rest. Your age may allow you to do much or less. Once the funds are there, have a team to delegate to. I suggest a part time team until the funds are there for full engagement that comes with much labour-related responsibility.

'MUYIWA OSIFUYE

You will do well with a list of daily tasks written out by you. Start with the most difficult item and cross through them as you get them done. There are days, you won't complete them, since you are not an inanimate robot; but do strive. Simply go back to continue, as new ones are added every evening.
A list pushes you. But when you do complete it, it can be heart-warming to do more. *You can get yourself a beer.*

All these efforts we make in the rat race of our existence are means to live quality life, while we are here. We should remember, as we pursue these goals, we should make life better for other human beings. Leaving behind a worthy legacy should be one of our guiding principles as entrepreneurs.

As you read on, you may see a semblance of the clichéd business plan. I have not said you should not draw up a basic or an elaborate business plan for the purpose of seeking financial sponsorship. But that is not my major thrust here as most small and medium businesses don't need that elaborate direction, when they are starting out.

While a business plan may be compulsory and useful for some start-ups, I have discovered some do not need it, at the beginning.
Just follow *Nike's*™ slogan; *"Just do it"*

You only need an appropriate personality and good character for the demanding business world. You need to quickly develop an effective business system, good innovative ideas, financial discipline and a considerate human resources system.
All these must be supported by continuous marketing of your offerings. These are the pillars in my reckoning that will ensure a successful business reaches maturity eventually.

In business, the unseen will rare up their ugly heads, it may not mean you are a bad decision maker. The lessons learnt here, is that external factors could influence your business. You will need useful insights from other sources. Because you can't simply know it all.
This becomes more important especially when you are under stress, when a quick solution might become elusive. While you might reach out for help, be careful that the company's secrets are not mistakenly divulged to those you seek assistance from.

Let me digress a little bit here...
Some neophytes in business, nursing erroneous thoughts, may think that founding a business, automatically turns them into being an Entrepreneur. Sad to say, that many start-ups owners still carry on with the employee mindset. Ultimately they get disappointed and confused about why things are not working.
The business lies comatose or dies.
The Entrepreneur has a different world view from that of an employee.

Before I wrote this paragraph, I was feeling slightly sleepy, so I decided to do a two-minute slow-exercise. I had to refresh as I have deadlines to meet. It is tough on the spirit and body. But you can always relax later and pamper yourself.

If you don't get your acts right, you may blame the good idea you had planted but not nurtured very well. You could erroneously blame the external factors, as a reason for failure. I am not saying that is not possible. But we need to check ourselves and our businesses too.

While rushing to start another business idea, you could meet yet another roadblock and retrace your steps back to the earlier one. So you need to know what it means to be an entrepreneur, to save the business and possible personal agony. Once done right, as I have conversed throughout this book, there will be plenty of time, to enjoy yourself even as you keep tab on the business.

Talking about your presence and that of your business with regards to government, governance and policies as both can't escape their influence.

In many parts of the global economies, the country runs most of the affairs of their citizens, even though the most obvious is governance through the platform of politics.
Many countries cannot supply all the needs of the market place because of many inherent restrictions in governance and the financial world. These would include the bureaucracy and the adequate manpower and skills that are needed to provide these services or products.

Therefore, most government establishments may not succeed as profit oriented institutions. This runs in conjunction with the fact that, there could be lack of commitment on the part of the public servants. This may not be as high as those found in the private sector.

Therefore, it is natural for you and I, to be poised to help the society, by rendering quality services; to produce relevant products the society needs in exchange for rewards. Because of this opportunity given to the populace, it is assumed going into business is simply a straightforward and an-all-comers affair.

Failure and successes have been experienced, by business people who came before you and I. As I have said, I have had my own fair share of mistakes - nothing to be proud of - despite huge and useful lessons learnt.

When you make a repeat effort and discover you have exhausted all the tricks at your disposal, and nothing is moving positively, it is time to abandon that idea and try something new. It might look like a drastic action but you have the consolation that, you didn't rush to such a conclusion.

Let me share briefly, a personal experience when I closed a branch of my eye clinic business.

It was my first, opened in 1994. I had known before opening at the first location, that the area did not have a growing population of my target consumers. At that time, that was the only available opportunity for me, to transfer my dream of entrepreneurship from paper into reality.

But I had a plan "B" in case what I envisaged, came up to be true. My plan was that I would immediately save money from the sales, to get another more befitting location elsewhere, to serve as a new head office. This became a reality despite much personal pains and inconveniences I went through.

Over time, this initial place had sales dwindling despite heavy discounts I introduced. Fewer people were stepping in. I did not panic as I had already paid for another space elsewhere, after saving for about fourteen months.

I got the second place to come on stream. For a while, I moved between the two as a consultant, to save cost. I eventually closed my first branch and started a different business at this first location - a business which had far more opportunities in that locale.

Although that didn't last long. It was due to my naivety about handling human nature at that time and some unavoidable challenges. However lessons have been learnt, thankfully.

There is a natural tendency to romanticize the first set of ideas that comes to mind. Don't fall for that emotion. Look at your ideas objectively. This used to be a personal weakness. I have overcome it. Today, it may appear as if I am slow but I am just being painstaking while I respect the urgency at hand, more so, as one gets older. There are times, when there are exceptions though, when the risk of failure is very minimal - you take action.

The business world does not thrive on sentiments. Don't belittle some ideas or hints that may seem as a no-brainer. Such may be your saving grace. In business, you might be surprised, when you look closer, that there is more to it than meets the eye. You would discover very latent and subtle issues, which equally need our attention for success.
Despite your business experience and professional academics, you must still be circumspect. That is another realm. The business schools don't teach that.

Lastly, private businesses form the bedrock of the economy. Opportunities must be discovered so that one could serve the various market needs, which include government institutions as well. Referring to the latter, the majority of the equipment used by the military, including the very sophisticated ones; these are the results of the creative minds of the civilians, working in their labs.

The scientists who hunch over their tools, coming out with new discoveries are the players who serve various arms of government. Such services could also be rendered by the ordinary folk, down the street, who works on a simple idea to solve a problem. That is an entrepreneur.

2
The Marketing Plan

Here I will share what you should be doing if you have already started your business. Also if you are about going into business, you will see some nuggets of ideas you should put in place before spending any money.

Get a paper and pen for your check list.
You will test your idea with a realistic set of objectives as follows:

Identify possible consumers, their behaviour, unique needs and size of their population.
Have you identified alternative products or services that can give you a clue about them?
Where and how they want to be served?
What is the true picture of their logical and psychological orientation?
The price they would easily pay for your offering.
How and where you can get their attention and feedback for the new idea?
What is the best way to present the product and service, if the idea is "truly" needed?
How much of your expendable resources (money, time and manpower and energy) are available to have a quick test?
These and more…

In your strategic plan, you must know your customer, the price range you want to sell, your cost structure and expected profit you desire.

°MUYIWA OSIFUYE

Your strategy must position your business at the middle or either of the extremes of the economic bracket. Will you be serving the low or the high or in between? As matter of fact you can haphazard a guess about the market's perception. You want to discover what your prospective consumers feel about quality and how much they readily would pay.

How do buyers of the Rolls Royce car interpret quality and what values do they place on such a product? In the same vein, why do some cheap chocolates as well as the expensive ones, sell differently at a profit?

Good marketers play on the psychological nature of Man. They can position a pedestrian product to look eclectic, if they will get away with it. Marketers are aware that customers cannot be forced to buy but by persuasion and seduction of the senses.

There are many tactics and tools available to get this done. But above all, be warned, if you lie about your offering, they will get to know and your business will suffer. So do not take the market for granted, when making promises.

Consumers are generally irrational in their buying decisions. We all are, on many occasions than not. Smart businesses position their products to trigger the emotion. So you have to discover what makes your target market tick while you produce an equitable product.

Granted that pricing may be elastic in some situations, but you may not be able to stretch it too far, at the two extremes.
If it is too low, you may make good sales. Likewise, if price is too high, you may not sell, as well. And you may make more sales by increasing or reducing from your current price, depending on your strategy. Pricing can be very fluid.

There are some products people don't buy because they perceive them to be too cheap, with the assumption of low quality. They may be wrong. It all has to do with perception and positioning of your product.

In fact, where it is appropriate, never give the initial impression to a prospect that you are desperate to sell. This needy approach connotes a low quality offer. If you can map out a scarcity tactic, working on behavioural pattern, customers may beg to be sold to at a higher price. It is a delicate act, so balance it well.

A single star and a five star setup may sell the same products differently. What is the difference, and what could be responsible? A lot.
It could be the ambience, location, relative safety, customer service and more.
A worthwhile after-sales-customer experience might allow your business to charge more. All these efforts go into your marketing plan and daily tactics to enable them become a reality, must be initiated from the beginning of the business.

In brief, now let us talk about discovering best ideas.
Let me give a personal opinion about lists of ideas that are bandied around as the only way to get good ideas. Everybody has these lists by now. Look at these lists but discover your own business ideas. And there several ways of doing that.
You can only draw up a good marketing plan or strategy on an idea that you own; an idea which you can tame and tailor to the specific needs of your earned customers.
A marketing plan involves your current and prospective consumers' strong needs, followed by you putting up a good business system in place to produce and to take care of an identified segment of the market which must be willing to pay.

°MUYIWA OSIFUYE

Your product can never be needed by everybody in the world except you are selling the air we all breathe now. So there is a need for market segmentation. I have made the term simple. Within a segment of watch wearers, there are people who prefer leather straps, metal straps and other materials.

It is much easier to go further down in serving a sub-segment like this, which is called a niche. But it must be done under a few conditions. Is that *'niche'* population large enough to accommodate your business and other competitors into the future? The niche must be able to feed your business for long term production.

Watch out, for trends that change. They don't announce themselves. And watch out when you are coming in, it might be too late considering all the money and other resources you want to deploy. On the other hand, you might predict a possible new taste in the future and therefore, you are out of the starting blocks before anyone.
But watch it; the big boys may come in to join. It is your being innovative that will save you. That's getting ahead of your customers' needs by continuous dialogue with them. A step ahead, always. Forget the success of the previous day. That is the secret.
All these must go into your marketing plan.

As a self-employed what you are bringing to the table in the world of enterprise, is that you have discovered a need, which a portion of the public desires and they would not hesitate to pay for. They will pay if your product or service meets their expectations.

Entrepreneurship is fundamentally an exchange of valuables between a producer and a consumer, while charting a course for future needs by the market.

There are occasions the idea might come from you, maybe due to a personal experience. It happens. An epiphany some call it.
Before you rush out to deploy all resources, you must validate or find out if a large portion of the market really wants it. If they don't, then don't bother, even if you like it. Look for something else.

It is not about you, it is about those who want to pay you for reducing their pains or making their experience much better, than what is available in the market place.
Prospective and current customers love themselves more than you. Consumers care less about the seller.
However do note that some ideas are embraced by consumers without prior research or simple survey…just an instinct thing. The risk is on you if you take this route and you get the reward if the idea is accepted.

How To Make A Million In Sales

Let me prick your mind about this popular thought, most of us have about making money. You might have thought sometime, about how to become a millionaire. But you wouldn't know how to go about it, to make an honest million ultimately? This is an open secret.
The answer is simple.
Sell something that "millions" of people would like to pay for. Keep your thought at bay, about going into exotic items that only the few rich can afford. That clears your mind and removes the confusion, right? Good!

Then deal with the most difficult assignment which is, to leverage on a network or create your own distribution network, to reach millions of consumers *over time*.

Pick an idea that is repeatedly used, and seemingly low in price.
Coca-Cola, Pepsi and other beverages always sell. You now know one of the reasons behind their perennial success.

°MUYIWA OSIFUYE

Your little margin - after deducting expenditures - when multiplied in millions of products bought over time, will ultimately bring you a million of your currency or more. It takes time and patience but you will get there.

If you can't reach the millions, coordinate other service providers, who can't market their own products themselves. Become the middle man. Market their products and service to consumers and collect your fees, from the consumers and providers (as well). Replicate the system across your country. *Buy a nice cuisine to celebrate your first million.* Then scale and repeat the process.

Soar above competition by adding something else, in a combo to your idea, to sell easily. Beverage companies sponsor shows you know. It is a game of numbers. Look out for other opportunities. They are out there.

Mostly the impatience in people and their ego may not allow them to see the humble ideas - the gold and the diamond in the rough.
Reserve a day, every week to think widely and conjure scenarios to test the possibilities of serving humanity in exchange for monetary values.

A few software application developers have become millionaires this way, in a very short time. You don't have to be one. Outside the digital world, you could solve other problems, simple in nature that affect mankind.
If you are lucky, where copyright and patent laws are enforceable, your business can climb to the zenith.

Authors who write content, that moves the soul, with good marketing, could sell in millions, even at a low price. *As you are reading this, tell your friends about my thoughts. Would you?*

Where To Get Your Customers?
There are basically two approaches you will use to get customers to know about your business. Not all business types may work with the advice I am about to give which is as follows:

It is either you go to them, where most of them aggregate and tell them how they will benefit from your service.
The second method is to do what will make them come to you.

You can qualify this better by doing both. You can also leverage on partnering with other businesses that serve your ideal prospective customers.
But this will not be free. *"Nothing goes for nothing"* - in recommendations and referrals by others. But this is one of the fastest ways to get patronized. *Support or endorsement from a big boy or big girl...the Influencers' quickens your publicity.*

Several tools and marketing techniques will be used.
Giving out flyers, posters, reaching out and listening very well to target prospects and groups.
Giving out freebies and partnering with successful business owners, within the community. You can apply same thoughts to an online business. You need to do a lot of legwork to reach out. You schedule your appointments on a daily basis to do this forever.

You may even do direct marketing by writing about your business benefits and making such available to your target audience.

On the other hand you may create a modest public event or awareness for your new service to attract your prospects to you.
Today, most discerning customers make up their minds faster this way, when you allow them to test your offers first. Signposts on your office

door, newspapers adverts, and flyers dropped at different locations; all these will be part of your pleasant shout out.

For new businesses, I am not too sure you can afford to try radio or TV at the earlier stage because of relative high cost.
Your business might benefit by setting up shop at a location where the majority of your clients will be found. You can leverage on such businesses and asking for a slot at their locations if you can afford the latter. Otherwise you may pick a corner piece in that area.
As an illustration, if a location is popular for men' wears, would you consider having a small gym in that area? Look around for such a synergy.

For an online business, it demands more work and resources, due to the huge number of related internet based businesses.
The secret to attention for an online business is promotion for visibility as against physical business which is location. Either of the two orientations must seek attention both; online and offline.

One of the fastest ways to meet with your prospective consumers is to simply advertise online. It costs money but if the content of your webpages or website are very beneficial, you could start making money much faster.
Also don't forget to do the real world in publicity. This works in tandem. For the latter in your community, a gathering of a small event sponsored or run by you must be taken into account. Your website or physical office may be picked from such an event. The word of mouth will do the rest, albeit slowly.

You will also want to be very active on the social media platforms. If you can't do it, hire somebody to do that for you at the right time and continuously. Personally, I am not really inclined to blogging but having fresh presence is needed on the web, no doubt about that.

From time immemorial, the human population have congregated at different arenas, as trends change; do locate all those watering points. Where your business can afford to be seen, be in their face. Set money aside for such. Try to measure return on such investment for attention for all outlets.
You may have to do all this yourself to save cost. But over time, it is much effective to identify and outsource these services. But make sure you define your objectives with them. And the results must be measurable; otherwise you won't know how effective your campaign is.

Reappraise all efforts on a periodical basis. Get to hear feedbacks from these potential customers and make adjustments to your offerings as desired.

Lastly, remember you must see it as a duty to bond with your customers. Design a proper plan to regularly reach across to those you have served and the hesitant ones. Do not see your interaction with them as a one-off dealing which is an error in selling. I had made this regrettable mistake in the past. Always have something beneficial to communicate with them Marketing is forever.
Learn from Coca-Cola and others in that ilk. Set aside part of your monthly budget (if need be) no matter how small, to seek and bond with customers. You may not see the returns immediately but your brand awareness is out there.
There is always a subtle payback time.
Do not let your business fade away from your customer's memory.

3
The Organizational Plan

It is important you pause very well, for a while to ask yourself about the ultimate vision you have for this baby you are about to give to the world.

You will ask yourself;
what is the vision for this business on a long term basis?
What is expected to be its mission?
These are very broad questions which demand good answers. It is only you that can answer these questions. I mean it is your duty to paint the picture of this business with a vision as you deem fit.

Oh yes, you may be thinking, the business is still young. But it is the vision that you have set aside from onset that guides the business ultimately.
For example, there are things you may not want the business to be involved in. Of course that is not to say that such goals that are set cannot be tinkered with - when necessary - over time.

Vision may look static but can be amended because of unforeseen circumstances. For instance, if you were to start a transportation business to move products, wouldn't you also embrace a wider vision for transportation in its entirety?
Beyond the products, you may want to include transportation of human beings (that is, passengers) once you have the opportunity and resources, should you be interested in the future.
I want you to have a basic projection of what your business goals should be and how to achieve them on a short term basis.

Write a single-page plan of how to get all these things done.
That is your organizational plan…

But for now, as a starter and being self-employed, you don't need 50 pages of content to get you going. As a matter of fact, plans do change. Therefore you can modify what you have written down. So don't be hard on yourself delaying and thinking of writing an elaborate business plan. A single page will do.

Building a business into a system of activities that meets its founder's objectives demands proper organization of all inputs. Most importantly, cash in the bank as against much profit on paper is the way to go! And of course, ensuring good customer satisfaction.

We are talking about managing the enterprise, your team, your customers, various external agents, and the nuances of unpredictable experiences. This will also include you as a human being. Your mindset and role you play as a leader.
You have a life to live and likewise the business you have also set up. All these must be organized and planned to make your living a worthwhile experience, as you traverse this earthly journey.

You will start with a vision from onset - a strategic pathway.
It answers all the, *"why"* and *"how"* questions, after you have validated a workable business idea.

You start with an overall plan for the business – a bird's eye view. Your business strategy is the tool you use to achieve your goals and objectives. *(This is the grand scheme of things you want to undertake.)* So it is a broad plan of sorts. They are written down. Then you deploy your tactical activities and the operational steps (these are done on a daily basis).

And you must know if a particular strategy is merely a waste of time, unrealistic or not.

The resources or the opportunities may be inadequate; this may prevent you, from hitting your goals. Strategies in that wise, cannot be cast in stone as goals may change.

In other words, before you to design your battle plan, confirm that your goals are realistic and they can be served within your innate capability. For instance, if you desire to become the president of your country, your present situation, interest and networking over the years in your life and in the political arena should have shown such possibilities. Otherwise, if you are not so positioned, no matter how lofty your vision for the country is, you wouldn't hit the mark.

Strategy is a long term plan and it takes into consideration, concise but rationalized milestones. These milestones are staged for the short, medium and long term time-frame, subject to the vagaries of many factors.

Have you noticed on the walls of some organizations, plaques plastered on the walls, spelling out their mission and vision statements? Many staff members in such organizations may not even be able to recall them. But what start-ups need as a compass for direction, in these days of globalization, is to respond to new trends and nuances of the market. This should be part of your vision.

The market is so dynamic, that words imprinted permanently on plaques may become suddenly impracticable and obsolete before you know it. The business climate changes very fast these days, while old dogmas break down, irrespective of the economic bloc of where the business is situated.

Start the business. Nurture it. Let the world have a feel or smell your garlic or rose, thereafter they would make up their mind if they badly need your product or not. Your internal culture is what the business will exhale to the market. *It's better to work on the latter, always.* Your coined dogmas can follow later.

Your strategy must be written down before undergoing any action plan. It is like a compass or a road map which guides the business. Entrepreneurship is akin to a sustained battle. You must plan to win most of the time. Let your conquest be more than the losses. Therefore you need an overall view of strategy.

Now let's go deeper with a few questions to reflect upon - looking broadly at this entrepreneurial journey.

What should be the outlook of your business?

What should be the path to take, to the – shifting - *Promised Land*, which is our set of objectives?

What are the reasons you considered for starting the business?

What are the middle grounds between you and the business…free time for yourself and family?

What do you really want for your life and your existence?

If you are a manager of a business, what are your expectations for your life, even if you are not the founder? And many more…

It will be wasteful to move around like a lost cork, bobbing up and down on water - pushed around by waves.
You must see yourself as a captain of a ship or an airplane aiming to get to its desired destination. Determining how long it will take you to get that destination is where your plan and full conviction come into play.

'MUYIWA OSIFUYE

You must believe and develop a business system to achieve your goals. I can tell you that the goal posts could move, unexpectedly.

Checking up on your assets and resources you have and being realistic about your situation is very important. You must also know your strength and the opportunities out there that you can tap into.

Do not run away from your weaknesses but resolve them. A one-eyed sailor can still sail to his destination.
You must be cognizant that there would be threats of turbulence. Unless you can keep the ferocious wind still and possibly walk on water to get to your rendezvous, you must devise means of minimizing these inevitable challenges. Otherwise, the business suffers. Lookout for all the assistance, you would need. Life is not a bed of roses.

When you set out, you must have milestones written out; determine the time frame of attainment. Please do not put the route you want to take in your head. Write it out and keep it where the members of your team can have a glimpse of them, including you.

Endeavour to reflect on them every day, as the promoter or the leader. This attitude stimulates your action and activities. It keeps you on your toes, on those days when things are not going as planned. It refreshes your energy; same it does to the energy of the management. This is the essence of the strategic plan. It is as simple as I have described.

For instance, assuming you want to be producing *fashion* belts for sale; your plan - as written – could look like this:
Decide if you want to be making 200 belts monthly, for the next two years.
Decide on the number of shades of colour, five or more.
Will special buckles be added from the sixth month based on your

modest market demand and funds?

You may want to add complimentary product lines. These could be leather wallets for men, from the same material, once a loan has been cleared or enough cash has been set aside.

Having established this plan; be cognizant of some rough rides that may threaten your course.

They can come in the least expect form. Learn how to look with your telescope at the far distance to appraise situations beforehand.

At the same time, as part of your operational activities, you will also need a magnifier to look at the tiny distractions close to your skin. These are the ones, we do not see naturally. Is it your trouble with your core staff or your sole supplier who is about going bankrupt?

Despite having faster inertia, some small businesses can capsize easily. You must come to a quick decision, to manage troubling situations that may build up.

Big businesses might secure a few barges to bail out before the ship goes under completely. The advice given here is easier said than done but you must keep your successful enterprise afloat. Never, ever allow it to capsize. When you have done your best, you will know.

Organizational Structure

One of the elements of achieving your goals is also to put up a structure. If I may ask; what do you need to safely climb to the top of a roof? You will definitely need a ladder or a manifold. This is the tool you will need to achieve this kind of aim.

In business you will need an organizational structure. This is a unique internal network of different activities manned by your team. And they tend to be different in many businesses, influenced by their business strategy.

°MUYIWA OSIFUYE

The popular units that make up a simple structure are, finance, marketing, human resource or personnel, operations, production. They can be further divided into subunits as the need arises. Newer names are now given to them and to the head of the units. Interrelationships amongst them are readjusted for efficiency. An organizational structure would change over time as strategies change. Either flat or hierarchical in nature.

Generally speaking, in the traditional sense, the bigger the structure, the more specialized and more efficient each sub-unit would be.
A smaller structure could be by design, but it must meet with the objectives of quality in all ramifications.
A young company that suddenly finds itself, doing big business must alter its structure. Adjustment has to be made to enable it meet its new obligations in a timely manner, to its customers and other stakeholders. The stakeholders would include the staff, investors, government agencies and others.

Having said that, you simply don't modify the structure - but for good reasons and available resources. This is one of the reasons, scaling up of an organization must be well thought out and planned. It is better to operate at a relatively smaller size that your company can optimize very well.

There are companies that choose to work under the radar because of competition, especially if the idea can easily be copied. They may eventually come out for strategic reasons after they have locked their customers into their beautiful services. I am into such a business presently.
Some pursue this strategy to avoid the competitive reaction they might get from the bigger players, who would simply suffocate them out of business.

When the structure is in place, especially for big organizations, the different units should be allowed to do their job, with minimal intrusion. Yes, I used the word, intrusion, deliberately because; in as much as no unit should be left absolutely without some supervision, your team will need relative freedom to deliver.
It is expected of the management therefore, that when these units are being setup, the right calibre of staff are posted therein. The units would be given a set of instructions with measurable objectives in line with the philosophy and vision of the company.

Some founders would want to be directly involved in the day-to-day activities of their companies; therefore, a simplified structure might be put in place. It may be a chain of command that is very short, with an almost direct communication with the factory floor.
This is unlike some big companies that mimic the military command structure, where the foot soldier is far from the commanding general. So different industries work best with what they deem right, hoping it is appropriate though.

However, do note that the traditional structures associated within an industry could change with time. The game changers may be due to new knowledge, life style changes, the dynamic information (technology) and the social media.

If you study these scenarios very well, it may throw up an opportunity for you to work smarter and deliver more effectively. On the other hand, they could be a threat to your company's long term existence. That's a lost battle for the perennial conformist, who refuses to discover that the juicy cheese has been moved elsewhere. So watch out now.

Despite the prevailing style of structure peculiar to your industry, study it again. Within your industry, research if going against the norm - within the laws – can give you a huge edge. That is changing you operational strategy, from the common practice, to satisfy clients better and become more profitable.

The obvious point to make is that many people, including some entrepreneurs are used to popular conventions. You don't have to follow the crowd of conventional wisdom.
So that is your weapon, go against such, in a smart manner. Quietly develop and deploy a new strategy in your industry. As a matter of fact, an entirely different industry can give you an insight. You can modify such to solidify your business, for a much improved customer experience. This might make you huge profits, attained at a faster pace than through the well-known, popular route.

Legal And Regulatory Requirements
There are some businesses you can start without necessarily registering a legal entity at the beginning. Ask people in your industry about how much you can delay this in your country.
Before starting a new business, you will be looking at the legal and other professional requirements, which must be in place, before you open shop. It is ultimately to your advantage not to run afoul of the laws of the land. This allows you to freely serve the market, without any apprehension and hindrance.

Much work is done to get a business off the ground; therefore you would not need any distraction from the relevant authorities. In that wise, it is smarter to process and collect the necessary papers, permits or licences.

Types Of Business Formations
Businesses come in different forms and entities. They include the sole proprietorship, the different types of partnerships, the private limited

companies and the public limited companies. There are other sophisticated legal business entities, like holdings.

A good small-business lawyer would guide you, on the most appropriate choice to make, during the life cycle of your entrepreneurial journey. Do note however, that the most popular type of business entity is the sole proprietorship. Most people start from here. It has its advantages and disadvantages.

I am not too keen on the partnership type. When necessary, I'd rather I worked with a partner on a particular project, which is time bound. Partnership could be tricky. If you can avoid it, do so.
Considering certain advantages of combined skills, if you want to go this way; get a lawyer to document things; no sentiments at all. We all change as humans, you know.
And above all, beyond the initial excitement; study the prospective partner and your own personal orientation too. Do you share almost the same set of beliefs? It is a hunch thing. You have to feel it, to get it right. I personally left a joint management, on two occasions when I thought my partner was dodgy. On hindsight I came to be right. Though things were delayed for me in the actualization of my business, but I cherished my peace of mind, eventually.
Partnership must be a mutual agreement of the minds *with the hope you are not the difficult one.*
Lastly, look around your intending partner, if the influencers around him or her share the same vision with you or not. Troubles could come from these angle too.

Naming The Business
Many bother themselves so much about what name to anoint their business. A name can mean much but it is not absolute. Some successful

businesses have names that are so neutral, yet the consuming public has a peculiar impression and emotion about them.

Of course you won't use words that are insensitive to the culture of your market. The business is patronized because of a clear message and the quality of the customer experience as expected. This is what a name conjures in the mind of prospects ultimately; be it a good or bad image. But if you have the liberty, you may choose a name that says much about your product - no qualms about that. But don't waste much time if you can't find one.

Having arrived at your well informed business idea, you will be considering the name to call it, which you will need to register legally. Naming a business can be an exciting affair for many people. It is akin to birthing your own baby; naming her and watching her grow.
While it is true, that the name you give to your business may connote a particular image of your desire, watch how the public otherwise interprets it.
The perception of your company, in the mind of the public, is greatly influenced by the totality of what your company projects. This will include the calibre of your team, your offerings and how the business is positioned to the public.

Imagine, you sell pencils and choose to name your company,
 "The Pencil Enterprise". Disappointingly, a business named XYZ, sells far more pencils than you. It could mean, in this case, your name has not done much. The descriptive name is just a bonus. You need to do more for more customer acceptance, to increase your sales.

Remember that the generic names of most companies do not reveal their offerings. It is the general consumers' experience that matters.
Your brand or what the public makes of the business is what will be most

important factor on the long run. So whatever name you call your business, ensure it does not confuse your target. And be watchful of the prevailing culture of where you operate.

There comes a time, a successful name becomes generic. Google is now a new lexicon for online searching.
A brand is eventually formed. Branding like this, takes years to register in people's mind. Deliberate efforts are packaged into quality service delivery and good image. Even as individuals, our names may conjure different emotions amongst friends and detractors.
So pick on a relevant name but work on your overall delivery and perception. Your character and the personality of the business matter. Either for good or bad, an enterprise can be influenced by the owner himself, the employees and the words the consumers project to the public. Be aware it is a connected world we have today, where any type of news can be delivered in a jiffy.

The Underground Kingpins

You may not believe it, you may have to give cognizance to some infamous underground entities, where you want to set up shop or operate. In some countries it is only after you have taken care of these nefarious groups before your business can have a breathing space. Dig deep to find out, if there is anything like that in your locale or country. They are never easily known to be in existence by a newcomer.

Building For Performance

A business ought to have a life of its own, even as it is nurtured by Man. And anything that has life can thrive. It can also die if it is not taken care of. Watch out for influencers, so mentioned above, as they can bring about the extinction of a business, if they are not well managed.

As your immediate environment might influence your business decision;

this brings to mind a friend of mine who was into a computer related business. He had many computer units used by his team. They had just moved to this yet another, more spacious location. To say the least, each time they resumed at work, on most Monday mornings, most of the computers needed several rebooting.

Mind you, the place was not spooked.
The culprit? They later found out... to be rats!
Each weekend, the rats had ample time, to eat into the network cables. On the advice of the pest control guys, my friend had to relocate his business, from that vicinity, after three months. Meanwhile he had spent much on some infrastructure, planning to settle down for the long haul to make good money.

Let us look at a micro-entrepreneur-which is a one-man army outfit. Not surprisingly, at the beginning, the organizational structure may be embedded in him alone. It should be quickly noted, that tasks can be outsourced to affordable freelancers, both online and offline.
A single man or woman can set up like a bigger enterprise in this wise. Business models keep on changing for good, thanks to technology and new thinking.
Inside of him are domiciled such basic departments of an enterprise. These will include finance, production, sales and marketing. When other people come on board, new units can be added, depending on the size of the company.
There could also be your own small research and development (R&D) section, which is very much noticeable in big companies. At your level, that would be essentially, your overall but dynamic marketing outlook of current and prospective consumer changing behaviour.

As a company gets more established, growing in size, it will need a structure to make it work. Different activities are set apart for efficiency

and effectiveness. It is organic; it is gradual, bit by bit...
A structure evolves within due to a natural demand for it, as company passes through its life cycle. How tight the structure would be, is determined by the management and constrained by the overall strategic plan of the enterprise.

For example, some businesses choose not to scale beyond a particular level of growth. They simply choose to offer limited services or products. Therefore your structure would be leaner than a conglomerate that has much bigger strategic plans, aimed at playing across the world, with multiple products. This will result into units, departments, divisions, semi-independent branches scattered across the world.
There are conglomerates that boast of different managing directors under a global group chief executive officer.

The Organogram And Relationships
Now, how do we put together the different structures and size of an enterprise? The so-called organizational chart... also known as the *Organogram*. It is a graphical but a functional representation that shows the command structure in an organization.
They are nodes of responsibilities and interactions amongst all of them. It shows the most important supervisors and officers up to the head of the group. It shows the interrelationship of various units, officers and structure of delegation of duties.

In the nuclear family, it is most likely, the flattest it can be. The kids have direct access to each other and to their parents. Is yours different, my reader? *Send me an email.*

The Organogram comes in different shapes and complexity. In big organizations and the military, the chart takes a pyramidal shape. The overall head is at the top of the pyramid, with increasing number of officers sharing power as you move towards the broader base.

However, the flat structure nearly puts all the important officers on the same level, just below the chief executive. Many organizational charts pick their shapes in between these two extremes as they deem fit. The flat or the hierarchical pyramidal shape is not just a fanciful exercise. It is a very thought out decision, based on the strategic vision of the business.

There are companies, in periods of crisis; the structures become very fluid and flexible. The C.E.O. may have to come down from the pinnacle, to work with officers at a lower level.

For some conglomerates, who are accustomed to the pyramidal shape, decisions can be very slow, when compared to companies that are closer to the flat shape. The highly hierarchical are the very bureaucratic organizations. Playful as they may look, these shapes can affect the fortune of any organization in either direction. Try the military structure in your family and see what happens in one week.
Today, modern tools of technology have altered the traditional shapes in many companies.

Changing the structure is not a playful thing, even if the power is vested in you as a chief executive officer. The shape arrived at, must emanate after painstaking strategic plans. It must serve different relationships between staff, customers and other external groups the business deals with, while taking cognizance of the overall objectives of the enterprise.

As you enter the business world, you must accord a business as a separate entity, even if it is under your influence. The word "business", sounds like, being "busy" which must be optimally done but with smart results. The sole aim is to exchange items of value between the producer and the consumer.

Creating A System

An entrepreneur should be able to build a business as a system. That is an easy way to sustain a profitable enterprise into the future and in the absence of the founder.

People create the system to drive a business. It is not the other way round.

A system is made up of the processes you have put together, the seemingly connected acts and activities, which are adjusted over time, to serve a strategic purpose. A system may evolve slowly, as trends and time may demand a little adjustment here and there. This is not to say, a system must be altered every time. Therefore, if these aforementioned are not giving expected results, action and activities are faulty somewhere.

A bad system is a reality. For example, it might just be a single sloppy staff who chooses to be a cog-in-the-wheel of progress. An unreliable supplier can also throw spanner into your works, at short notice.

Find time to audit all the various aspects of your input, both human and other resources. This is more frequent in the airline industry, to avoid disaster and losses in all ramifications. You do check the oil in your car, don't you?

You need to identify the input, the innards (that is the processing mechanism) and ultimately the output of the system.

We could break it down as follows:

Whatever comes into a system are the inputs. This will include government regulations, prospective customers' needs and suppliers. This will also include the calibre of our staff, the fallouts of competitive environment, the nuances of the general public, the peculiarities of the immediate environment and beyond. These and other factors, an enterprise has to contend with.

'MUYIWA OSIFUYE

In the midst of these factors, your business is expected to process any combination of these factors, towards a desired output. The outcome is expected to be agreeable with the expectation of many. They will be made of your customers, your staff, your investor, government regulations, the environmental and the general public and more.

Since no business exists in a vacuum, the aforementioned must be very well managed, to ensure success within the society. Ensure that the internal mechanism is well tuned, and then mistakes will be very much minimized. Challenges are bound to come but the business will be better placed to manage them.

It is a tough job; businesses go through to survive to maturity. Once the requirements of each unit are partitioned and treated, then, managing them becomes easier. You can run the system like a machine but it must be well tuned. So watch what your business eats, ensure the internal organs are well taken care of, for an outcome of a well-nourished body.

If the processed output is extended a step further, by providing an icing on the cake to the clients, be rest assured the world would beat the path to your company's doorstep.
But be careful, don't grow too fast if your present resources can't cope, including your team's readiness and measure of skill.
Your business philosophy is about service, whether your outfit is dining table-bound, in the garage or domiciled in offices across the world, with diverse workforce.

Modelling your business in a system format makes for better appraisal and objectivity, to know where the business stands. A business system helps in determining quality, efficiency, effectiveness and recognition of milestones which can be subjected to measurement and standards. Such a system will reveal successes and failures and steps to take, to manage each scenario, when they occur. If every activity within and outside your business is not set up for measurement, the business is being cheated from attaining excellence, in optimum usage of material and human resources.

Managing Employees

Having identified your market properly, you ask yourself if you alone can get the business started or you think you need other helping hands. Be very careful here before you consider employing a staff. A lot of issues must be resolved.

Will the staff have a very frequent task to do on a daily basis?
If the answer is a *No*; I will suggest you get people to work for you only when there is a task at hand.
Establish prior contacts with these persons or individuals, so that you can call them out when you need them. You may have enough capital but don't rush against the rule of logic of enterprise, that is you spend only when it is very necessary. When you have the opportunity, you optimize your capital and other resources. But ensure your services and the qualities of the products are not compromised. You can't be too stingy in service delivery. Weigh things out!

If you are very convinced that it is a business that you must have people employed, from the beginning, then strive to keep aside about three to six months salaries prior to starting. Then go ahead and bring them in.

During the recruitment process and the interview, let the candidates know exactly what they are going to do. There should be no surprises from either of you.
An experienced business owner could help you out by joining you at the interview panel - maybe for a small fee – for a second opinion.

'MUYIWA OSIFUYE

Do realize that we human beings are the most difficult resource to manage in any business.

Document the job description and let the staff have a copy of this on resumption of duty. This is very important. Quickly design and make available a job manual. Your team must be aware of the tasks that go with each duty post. This would become in useful for all sorts of appraisal later on.

The employee must work under probation between 3 to 6 months or so before you deem him confirmed or ask him to go if he can't measure up. Abide by the agreement and your country's labour law.
Harbour no sentiments when you have to let the person go. You will get to know why, when you read much further down. It may be good for him and your business for him to go. He could be a super staff elsewhere but many employees won't own up for their own good. That is human nature. This is very crucial.

Jobs should not be personalized around a team member. That is a recipe for failure in performance. The duty or job description should come first and the right staff should be matched accordingly.
For a young small business, you can employ a basic entry-level staff that you can train, to imbibe your organizational culture. If it is feasible in your industry – delay employing overqualified personnel since they are already used to a different working culture, possibly coming from a bigger establishments than yours. And they are equally set in their ways.

Bring such calibre of staff in, only when very necessary. (You will know as your industry and your goals would dictate).

Do not be in a hurry to hire but don't waste time either to let a disgruntled or uncooperative staff go - after due diligence.

(Many years back, a new venture of mine collapsed before my eyes because of sentiments I had for my two old staff who should have been asked to go). If you have to fire: follow your labour laws and prior agreement.
If your business gets sick and dies, nearly all the employees fraternizing and praising you as a nice boss would leave.
It happened to me, more than once.
You will feel betrayed, lonely and suddenly naked!

Even if the business is doing well, any of your staff could still leave based on their own best judgement. It is simply self-preservation at play – a free world. (The two above left on their own accord when they realized the ship had capsized. I couldn't stop them).
So don't get too sentimental, take care of your business too.

Of course being courteous to your staff is a humane thing to do. It is also expected that such gesture would translate to a high morale, with positive results for the business and good customer experience.

It is a delicate balancing act, managing human resources in any enterprise. There are theories and tools for guidance but there is also a place for a matured and emotionally balanced leadership.
It is not easy. It comes with well-honed social experience, critical observation and intuition.

You can't grow a great company alone. All I have said so far should be extended to other shades of people that your business must interact with in the public space.

In our contemporary times, an organizational structure could extend beyond the traditional physical format. You as an individual could put up a virtual structure using the Internet and other modern means of technology to attain a bigger size and outlook.

This is becoming common today, where a business promoter may have his staff spread across the world. He may not have a physical interaction with his workforce. However, this model of structure may not be feasible for some businesses due to their peculiar nature.

Still talking about virtual structure, if your business allows it, you could arrange a workforce that can be sourced through popular internet websites. Some of those found online, will include *Freelancers, O'desk, Fiverr, Upwork, Craigslist* and looking around for others in your physical community. But ensure as in the physical world, you do your due diligence, when engaging their services, as well as giving safety considerations before divulging sensitive information.
Determine to get quality of service that is proportional to your budget and compare the deal and task with an offline specialist.
The reality is that this is a new innovation that will get entrenched into the future.
Use it without any regret but be cautious. It could give you a better leverage to cut more out of the market share from well-established and bigger companies, at a faster pace than you think.

Measuring Activities For Profitability

How do we then measure and control certain activities at the work place? It is a painstaking exercise, which is a bit demanding to set up at the beginning of any business. But it makes things much easier to manage throughout the life cycle of the business. The seed of accountability must be planted immediately.

If you have not done what I am about to share with you now; no matter the size of your business or longevity, please, pause and do it. You will gain more. I admit it is a struggle to do it.

So here I go…
No matter how trivial an activity is, put it in a written manual; how each task ought to be done and scored, with an appropriate marking system. You may need an external hand to develop these schemes for your business.

The Internet can be searched for free and affordable tools on different aspects of business activities. Just search for business tools for measuring x or y. Determine the best tool, based on further enquiry from current users (other business owners)
You may also develop your own measuring tool if your business is still at the infancy stage. It depends on how creative you are.

Some aspects of a business cannot be measured in physical terms; that is why the intuitive nature of an entrepreneur comes in, in managing a successful business. Measurements must be subject to many considerations.

For instance, there would be laid down written-steps, which must be followed in carrying out a specific task. As each is done, a check list must be ticked. Any missed step can be seen and taken care of.
Any sequence or step that is found missing must be investigated. This is the foundation of quality control, safety and effectiveness. Imagine you are a chef, an aircraft manufacturer or a surgeon or a baby sitter, all with clumsy attention to details, your output would be less than optimum.

If you were to ship a specific number of items to a client, the list must be ticked off as, *"attended to"* by the staff - for full compliance. If you are having a dialogue with a prospect, follow a predesigned routine and the set of questions. As the discussion ensues, you check the progress on your report paper, device, computer or what have you. Of course, some occasions would warrant few exceptions, when there is nothing to be written or ticked away.

A creative staff can use her discretion to save the day, despite the operations manual in front of her, to solve an unusual request. After-all, some creative pilots do save many souls, when routine instructions fail. There will be occasions where the scheme may be modified as nothing is absolute.

But it is better to have a scheme of deliberate actions for every task. It prevents chaos and ensures there is a smooth flow of business operation. A hint of this must be mentioned to prospective employees during the hiring process, so that they can be aware of it. Don't hide this from a prospective staff, otherwise he may be unproductive over time after getting the job since he didn't know what the task entails.

Profitable Business Models

Enterprises come in shapes and forms. Businesses use some known models or forms to generate profit in the market place. These forms could be pure or a mixture of bits from other existing models in another industry.

Once we have identified the needs in the market place, we can then consider the best business model to achieve our purpose of service.

I will hint at some identifiable models used by popular enterprises across the world.

Let us look at a few business models that can turn a profit.

Customers or clients pay for a service or a product. This is the asset that the business rests upon. This asset could also be tangible or intangible. An individual may need it or other businesses may lease or rent it from you.

If you don't have such an asset, you may buy it to start your business. But before doing that, do your due diligence about the financial returns and study the business deeply.

And if you choose to borrow, to acquire the asset, you need to work out your cost of capital (loan). Work out the arithmetic, to be sure that over a particular period you will recover your capital with profit, after other expenses. This exercise is what is called *the cost-benefit analysis*.

If you have an asset, that is idle, think about it. Someone may be ready to pay a fee for its use. Such an asset can be as wide as your imagination can run. They may be something you have expertise on and not necessarily physical in nature. The basic feature is; is it of huge value to another person or another business?

As a case in point, there are companies which rent out the phone numbers or emails of their clients. Assets are almost infinite. It depends on what you have, as an advantage. It may be a small physical item. It may also be an asset which is used a few times, by you or your company. Do you have an extra space or idle equipment? Remember, your own experience and expertise are assets. Your free time, too. What about your state of good health as well? Technology in form of an invention or patent can make you money too. The digital revolution with their applications, software and other related tools can change your fortune for good.

If you are not a programmer, but have good money, you can commission a geek to develop a tool so that you can market and sell. (*But get a good lawyer - trained in copyright laws - to take care of things.*)

There are applications to book taxis, to book hotel or airline ticket and so on... Computer and digital related ideas have made the world a better place to live.

'MUYIWA OSIFUYE

Good information sells. You can provide useful content that can turn people's life around for good. Find a system to monetize it. Create a following membership and establish a renewal platform.

You may build physical things from scratch, for rental and paid patronage. Most social clubs do this. The one that comes to my mind is the *Disney World*. Your successful rental model can be replicated, in more than one place. Remember to put a control system in place to prevent financial leakages of profit. Your book keeper or accountant knows how set up a good control routine to keep your funds in good shape. Ask him or her.

There are many websites, bloggers, authors that readily provide information. They make their content accessible to fee paying members only. You can also research about such information people are asking for and give it to them, where they are needed. This will generate traffic to your website. Advert spaces can be sold, as long as the traffic keeps coming, to benefit from your content.

This model is not exclusive to the Internet platform. It may be used in a neighbourhood, such as gyms and specialized clubs of interests. Establish activities that target a specific age group or demographics. Not everybody. Serve them with what they want as services. Indirect advertising can take place in such a space.

Look at the model of the business giants like, Google, or Yahoo! They provide search engines, free information and useful tools. Millions of site visitors come there like dehydrated animals to water. Advertisers bid to rent space on these sites.
The rental model is a good idea for laid back people.
For the introverted personalities and the elderly who have suddenly found themselves out of work but have enough capital can test the

waters with this business model. They could share their years of experience in form through newsletters or workshops. A hint of that is where people bid at such a high price, for a few seats, just to listen to the oracle of Omaha, Mr. Warren Buffet? This is about being blessed with a unique skill and experience. It means a business can be initiated, where you sell your *know-how*.

If you are not marketing or are not Internet savvy, you could partner with freelancers online or offline, to make your assets known to the public.
Some specialized skills and information are scarce these days, and I will quickly say that the years of experience of the unemployed – especially the older folks or middle aged, are equally needed by the younger folks, across all many industries and countries.
If you belong to this group of people, get assistance to market your expertise and make your regular income. There is so much you have in you. Note this.
Today, the unconventional routes to education and literacy are becoming more popular. Do not take your experience to the great beyond. You can impact millions while you equally smile to the bank too.

The stuff you have inside of you may appear inconsequential to you, but don't cheat yourself. Those skills you have polished over the years are in demand by others. Those who have a need of this experience would gladly pay you. They appear simple to you because they have become routine, but difficult or inconvenient to others to do. Do the marketing, locate your clients and serve to make your money!

Beauty Of Equipment Leasing
Another profitable model is through leasing. Leasing is similar to the rental system. Leasing is mainly applicable to expensive machinery, tools or equipment, that may be required in large numbers, to kick start a

business.

New airlines wet-lease aircrafts, rather than outright purchase.

The buyer or the owner of the equipment is called the lessor. The lessor produces the item or makes the purchase and leases it out to the user, the lessee, based on agreeable terms of usage, payback and lease duration.

I will mention two basic arrangements here. There are others. Nearly in all cases, the user pays certain fees on a periodical basis.

(A knowledgeable lawyer, accounting professional and a technician are needed by either party to iron out the contract.)

One type of an arrangement would be that the rental fees will be paid on the equipment while the owner (lessor) maintains the equipment.

This is equipment (operational) leasing as called.

Both parties determine if and when the equipment could be disposed of or not, at the prevailing market value.

The beneficiary (lessee) could be given the option to buy the depreciated item, at a mutually agreed price. Otherwise, the lessor, that is the legal owner may take the item away after the completion of the contract.

In a second arrangement, the lessor supplies the money to the user (lessee) to buy the equipment. The equipment is registered in the financier's name. The user maintains the item while still paying the scheduled rental fees. This is called financial leasing.

A few months or years down the line, the lessor, that is the legal owner may open window for disposal to anybody. A buyer pays a disposal price to the financier who relinquishes ownership.

As I said leasing arrangements vary. The two parties can create different arrangements. The details are in the contract. Due considerations are given to all costs, maintenance, the time frame of usage, the rental fee and other financials are involved.

Leasing helps the user to kick-start a business or a project in the absence of adequate capital. This business option is common in the transportation, engineering and other professional endeavours. Study your environment and other parts of the world, where opportunities for this business model are waiting to be tapped.

It is a business that you might set aside, while you hold on to your regular job as an employee. And it is also a good form of diversification, for a business that is suffused with extra cash. The equipment doesn't have to be really expensive for you to start this line of business. It is also a business opportunity to consider, if you have a good credit rating.

You can make the purchase of a highly needed piece of equipment and lease it to professionals. Let an expert work the financials out for you. And the deal must be firmed up, with a mutually agreeable terms of contract. Laws governing leasing differ in different countries.

Many professionals start their businesses by leasing part of the requisite equipment. This decision helps their starting cash-flow. On the side of the business owners, even when you have adequate capital, you may not want to tie down your money, on a singular piece of costly equipment. You can spread your starting capital. You can make outright purchase of big assets, when the business has appreciable cash reserve.
It is all about planning and applying common sense, because rendering a service is not about the acquisition of all the expensive equipment, at the beginning. That was the little trick I employed when I started my eye clinic in 1994.

Your Network: As Asset
Building a network to easily reach consumers is another profitable idea. Build a good spider web. The very popular online web in the likes of Amazon.com is well connected with merchants and producers! Consciously built or not, over the years, you could leverage your own

network. Such a network could be as an outcome of the activities of your business. It is inclusive of your interactions with various publics. Networks can stem from your personal contacts. Put them to good use.

Leverage on found networks to distribute products and services. Why is this an opportunity? Because there are many producers of services and products, that lack the means to reach the market place. A solid distribution network is always a big booster, for a new or an existing business.

If you are a man about town, you could leverage on this to introduce products or services to your exclusive contacts. They don't have to be your own products or services.

Brokerage is another business model that can yield good profit. The idea you can come up with can be as wide as your imagination can take you. Networking is a middleman's concept. Just position your business between two services in need of exchange. That is the rudimentary principle.

Gains In Value Chain

Forms of integrations I will describe here are examples of diversification, which could bring some comparative advantages to some enterprises. As you plan to venture into a business of your choice, go after a business model that, you have almost a complete knowledge about.
You know the input or raw materials and you also know about the end product, the outcome. You will decide if you want to do everything, deal with a portion or not. This guarantees less risk and a relative peace of mind. *I will explain further in the next sections...*

A full knowledge of the industry you want to play in gives better insight, during decision making.

A note of warning before you proceed; do your cost-benefit analysis with regards to your situation before you make the additional efforts. You might be better-off, to stay the way you are.

In some cases to be more profitable or to recover from loss, some companies cut off these extraneous activities. They decide whether to produce the raw materials, do the product or be involved in the distribution to customers.

Why Not Produce The Input?

Some multinationals that are into retailing, prefer to set up a whole division that also supplies the raw materials. This is common in food business which is inclusive of farming and grocery outlets.

A value chain is established from production to retailing. We also see this happen amongst eyewear retailers. They design and contract manufacturers, to produce their unique branded eyewear. Today, a one-man entrepreneur can tap into similar opportunities, of backward integration, that is, being in control of the input for the business. For instance, if you have adequate resources and the managerial capability, you could add a raw material production unit to your retailing. This is referred to as backward integration.

However, you must have ensured that, this gives your business a comparative advantage instead of buying the raw materials from another producer. Otherwise, a backward integration may not be all that rewarding, financially.

A welcoming advantage is that, backward integration keeps the business away from the mercy of your major suppliers. You can control many variables, which will include innovation, price, quality and timely delivery. It also gives you certain advantages over competition.

Retailing Your Production

Forward integration is when you make products that are much closer to consumption or as completed items to the end users. It is another way of being more involved in the value chain - down the line - and having additional control of that business.

If you are a producer of raw materials, you may extend your portfolio further into processing the raw materials. You could also set up a retailing machinery to take the finished goods to the consumers. You do this because, amongst other reasons, there is a need to take advantage of premium pricing. Quality and timely delivery, including competitive pricing, are some of the advantages of this strategy; to discourage present and future competition.

If you were to be a farmer, you could develop and own a network of distribution to sell your farm produce. People get to know your outlets, to pick your farm produce or the processed items you have made from your farm produce.
You don't have to own the physical outlets - *this is akin to the affiliate marketing concept found online.* Pay an attractive commission to those extra foot soldiers, where you can't be. You need the numbers to make the millions. Work the math.

You could also use the opportunity of your distribution network – if you own or lease it - to carry other non-competitive but complementary products to the consumers.
There are retailers who would want to pay for this leverage you have, using your distribution outlets.
The textile industry, fashion designers and other related businesses tend to have their own retailing outposts to ensure control.

How Entrepreneurs Reduce Risks?

The rich go for streams of income from more than one source. That is the reasonable thing to do to make additional money beyond your primary business.

Diversification is done basically to avoid risk associated with a singular investment. You don't want to put all your eggs in one basket.

Diversification might introduce new product lines, complimentary to the existing ones. You might go outside the business, using part of the surplus cash, to invest in other businesses.

Diversification is different from divestment. Diversification means adding yet another business to the existing one.

Divestment on the other hand, is closing down a line of business entirely, while you make a foray into another industry.

Nokia left the rubber and tire production industry, to go into cell phones manufacturing, which was very successful. We are not too sure about their next move as I write this, because of the struggle they are going through. It has been a rewarding experience until lately, where they have to face increased competition.

Many decisions in business must be subjected to the analysis of your own identifiable unique strengths, weaknesses, opportunities and threats, in all ramifications.

You dare not dabble into a business, without subjecting the project to these criteria. That is not to say, some individuals have not started and managed very successful businesses based on hunches.

You may choose to diversify into a product or service that compliments your primary business. Be on the lookout for opportunities, to serve your current or prospective clients, the more.

Since you can't do them all alone, you will need to bring on board a team to navigate this journey with you.

°MUYIWA OSIFUYE

One of the major reasons why diversification is useful is that not all your products are subject to the same vagaries of internal and external factors. The risks factor in each investment is relative and different.
To me, I have learnt that nothing in this life is absolute but all things are relative.

A well thought-out diversified portfolio of business ventures ought to give aggregate positive returns. The inherent risk in each venture must also cancel each other out, to ensure the resulting overall risk, is at the barest minimum. That should be your goal in your painstaking choice of any investment. When you are in cash, all sorts of people will come to you, to take some equity. Watch the lollipop, they promise you.

Diversification is a philosophy geared towards reducing the risk. All investments are risky. All are. This philosophy rests on the smart premise that one cannot be absolutely sure of the future of any investment or project.
Nobody can predict circumstances, the affairs of Man and nature into the future. So an entrepreneur should not have any choice, but to diversify, at least into another venture, once the resources are there. For those not interested in putting up a physical business, a portion of the cash could be in the stock market and other instruments. But all ventures carry their inherent risks, as I have warned.

There is a quote in investment which goes like this: the higher the returns, the higher the risk and *vice versa*. It is a known cliché in financial circles.
But one could devise means, through new technology or some creative imagination to lessen the risk. I am not talking about the insider trading of privileged information, carried out by a few naughty brokers and dealers in some parts of the world.

Growth As Mixed Blessings

There are several questions that must be tabled.
Why do you want to grow?
Which areas do you want to diversity into?
Are you aware of newer risks that are associated with aspiration for growth?
Do you have the resources to back up the growth?
Have your employees or team attained the needed skill or are they trainable to sustain this newly envisaged growth?
Are the members of your team convinced about the reason for growth? Do they agree with your new vision?
Will the growth expose your business to bigger businesses that now recognize your enterprise as an irritant to be quickly frustrated from the industry?
What are your plans that assure you of a solid foothold, in spite of these possible challenges?
There are some of the challenges associated with scaling up a business; as every size of an enterprise, has its peculiar challenges and opportunities. For every phase of planned growth, adequate preparations must be made, for the immediate and long term objectives.

If you do not have the competence or the resources to run a bigger company, it is better to maintain the status quo. Never joke with the concurrent quality of services in the name of scaling up.
Note this very important point.
Will the cash returns- both in speed and amount - when based on your increased total asset going to be much higher in ratio?
Be big only if you have the assurance for great customer experience and bigger cash!

Growth is good, but you need to squeeze every value from your assets – both tangible and physical. Relatively speaking, a smaller sized company may perform better with its use of assets. Such receives faster cash in the kitty with a much higher ratio of cash to asset. Many big sized companies struggle with these indices. Such big companies do fall in a big way when they cannot make more cash quickly despite the increase in their total assets.

Truly so, in some industries, restricting the business to a smaller size may not be advantageous on the long run. Competition in some industries may ultimately stifle life out of a business that chooses not to grow. Therefore, there would be a need to scale up.
In order to manage growth, it is advisable to move on at the most convenient pace for the company. Because if a company grows too fast, it may burn out. This is common in the absence of the very important resources, to sustain the new experience, with its peculiar challenges.

Multiplying The Business

A business idea that is scalable is a recipe for quicker and much higher revenue. Why is that so? Because of more sales can be made.
However some ideas cannot be replicated in huge numbers. Such an endeavour cannot grow beyond a certain point, irrespective of the efforts and resources that are deployed.
A budding entrepreneur must reflect on this fact.
Many people by choice remain small, that is not a crime. It has to do about the philosophy and goals of the founder. It is nothing to be ashamed about.

If you were the house painter in your neighbourhood; kill the thought of scaling. How much can you on your own do directly? If you want to scale the business, you can as well be a broker in that service. Get other painters across the city to be under your company which would serve your locale and beyond.

Your unique selling point might be the logistics of getting the right painter for a particular job, in a timely manner. Other complimentary products and services might be added to your offers. You pay your painters and other service providers by using the commission model and do the marketing and service improvement on their behalf.

But compare that to a software developer, whose products could serve millions across the world. A business can also be programmed for growth, if it has more outlets with standards replicated wherever they exist. The hotel business comes to mind in this aspect.

There are businesses or vocations that may not be scaled but would still give good returns. If the expertise of such an individual or business is unique or in high demand, then a much higher fee can be charged.

Those who would fall into these categories of exclusivity would be movie and music stars and creative people and high tech companies. Others are nimble fingered sought-after surgeons, highly inspired motivational speakers, deep fine artists and more. For their success, this comes with proficiency, smart marketing, persistence and a bit of luck, in that order.

4
The Financial Planning

Before we get deeply into this, let us consider integrity and character as invincible assets that can be in your favour when you lack physical money.

Your good character or personality can serve as a solid asset – the goodwill - in a competitive industry. Not many organizations as a matter of priority have developed this clout. Grants or credit lines are given to those who have proved to be men and women of integrity.

The terms of financing could be made more lenient, by a creditor, enabling you to implement your plans quickly. In the eyes of a supplier, your perceived integrity can also buy you time for your repayment schedule.
Therefore, do not play with your integrity. It can save your bottom line, someday.

Overall, your competence, capacity to optimize your resources at hand, in getting effective results is the hallmark of a respectable organization. These attributes, do not come easy but they are achievable.
They can serve as powerful financial currency. Just look around the world, there are still some genuine examples to emulate.

What Will Save Your Business?
Let us make a detour first, about the emotional discipline that is needed when handling cash and money.
Being frugal is a solemn phrase that all business promoters should imbibe

as a mantra, because it is always difficult to control money when it is available. And why is that so? Because money, in whatever guise it takes, to be in your hands as always - metaphorically speaking - *will quietly plead to be spent*. It is always tempting not to do otherwise with cash in your kitty.

Spend only when you are not in a knee-jerk mood. Do not go near your credit cash, check book or cash when you are experiencing extreme emotion, such as happiness or sadness.
Slow down for a while; be in control of your mind. Then you can make a better judgment, even if you want to celebrate after a windfall.
This is an aside from being stingy. It is about mastering your emotions. After a while you will get used to it, to spend wisely.

The process won't be easy as human beings needs are insatiable. The need to be like the Joneses is a very powerful stimulus, but we can muster the will-power to subdue the faulty dictates of our ego, to the minimum.

Most wealthy people use the money that comes to hand, to generate further cash through investments. It is after that, they could use a part of the profit from such to buy some luxuries. They recognize what is the seed-money and they don't eat the seed, they are patient enough for the harvest time to pluck a few juicy fruits while having their tree-of-invested-money being nurtured into the future.

They would rather wait, plant the seeds, nurture them to germinate and wait for the harvest time. Now they can pluck a portion from the abundance to eat. The cultivated farm will continue to yield into the future. Mastering the emotion of delayed gratification is one of the most difficult things to do by a material and egoistic Man, in our competitive world of today. Work hard. Enjoy the sweat of your labour with luxuries you desire but do it in a frugal way.

'MUYIWA OSIFUYE

It is good to be financially secured against life's eventualities, and come, they will. Do not fall into the natural temptation of the more money you make, the more you spend. That simply means you are stagnant and not growing.
Cash in your account does not mean that, it must be spent because it is there for the asking. Spend only when it is very necessary and on what is necessary. And how do you decide if and when it is necessary? It is only you that can tell.
And if you work with a smart and committed team in your business, they may help you come to a right business decision, in taking up projects and in your expenditures.

Some of us spend based on expected money from clients. That's risky and it is a bad habit. Agreed there are instances where it is advantageous to do so, because of an immediate benefit, and then you could.

A certain amount of money should go into a term-fixed savings account. The amount may be small, it doesn't really matter. It is about being financially disciplined.
Such funds could be rolled over and moved into a compound interest savings account eventually. Huge amounts of money benefit from compound interests. You can use the accrued interest on a yearly basis, as a passive income. The money set aside does not have to be a very high proportion of the income because inflation would reduce the value over time. But at least, since cash is king, you are not embarrassed at critical situation. The set aside cash is there for your picking and for your rest of mind.

You are actually building gradually, towards a target which partly might guarantee you, a peace of mind into the uncertain future for the business. Such funds could also serve as a backup to your business or personal life in times of crises when they choose to come up.

In fact when such a crisis crops up, it might be a test for your creative instinct before deploying cash. More often than not, we are more sober and creative when we are in lack. Could that be where the cliché, *necessity is the mother of invention*, came from?
So stretch that creative thought and when it is not working, you can then take a portion of your savings, to bail your company or self out. Note the amount taken and work towards returning the same amount, when the opportunities make it possible.
A small capitalized business cannot afford to be in a bad financial standing, because it can easily go under if it can't meet a simple financial obligation. A good financial base helps to stabilize things.

Do not chew more than you can bite - a bad etiquette at meal time - which could be likened to a business that rushes to grow faster than its finances and other resources could eventually cope with.
When you choose to borrow, ensure proper and realistic projections have been made. Aside unforeseen circumstances, you should be able pay all monies including charges, fees at the scheduled time of repayment.

When making financial projections, I will strongly advise that you play it safe. It is better to put on the pessimistic cap, even when all the signs presently show a positive outlook, before making up your assumptions. Don't fall in love with business plan templates. Be pragmatic.

Time is also a factor, which can be used to generate sales you need. You could delay to make the money to make the purchase for the business instead of rushing to borrow. However, it depends. Work your math out.

There are two scenarios you could consider when you need cash for re-investment in an on-going business. You either borrow the money with interest for immediate usage.
The other option if the urgency can be tempered, you can gradually bid for time as a factor, to earn the money. The latter tactic I normally utilize,

when I can negotiate for an extended time frame to pay for a piece of equipment. Using time as an element is a free asset, waiting to be taken by anybody if there is life and future ahead of your enterprise.

The Reality Of Franchise

Some people desire to go into business by not building their own system from scratch. That is cool.
But be careful when you go the franchise way.
Close-by, painfully, I see struggling franchises' outlets. Many closed shops despite physical refurbishments, yet customers are not coming. Sadly I saw the impending extinction of one or two of these outlets. The telltale signs were there.

In my part of the world moribund *fast-food* eateries have been turned into religious centers and rental halls for events.
Do not get me wrong; others have made a good success of this route to having their own business. But there is more to it. Get an expert in this field if you desire this route. And ask if the trend has passed.

I would define a franchise as the learned expertise from a business system of processes leased out - at a fee - to another party. After a long while, a very successful business would have developed an effective and an enviable system that could be replicated.
This could be an opportunity to earn additional income for the creator of the business model, few years down the line. If your business has reached that lofty height, you may choose to rent out, these accumulated knowledge to another party that does not want to invent a new wheel in your industry.

The buyer - the franchisee - needs to take note of other things, before

venturing into this arrangement. While you may pay the annual fees for these trade secrets, you also need to do more on your own, to let your own business outlet stand out. This is where from my observations many fail. Many go to sleep, waiting for the big-brother franchisor to give all directives.
I have a feeling the franchisors do get fatigued somewhere along the line and would not be able to help - directly - the large numbers of their franchisees over time.
That is the cold truth and a bitter one. That's human. Therefore, the way to go is to stand on the shoulders of your franchisor and use their know-how, to build upon and make your business profitable. You must plan how to serve your consumers, giving them the best experience wherever your business is located.

To survive into the future, you have to create your own additional marketing strategy aimed at your segmented consumers. The efforts by your franchisor, while it will transfer a seal of authenticity to your business, they tend to be too general.
The trade secret you pay for should give your business a better inertia. But prepare to do more.
Use the template given and their future trainings; use them as a stepping stone for improvement. Do not assume all you are given is the ultimate single pill, that would solve all business ailments that your own enterprise is bound to experience whenever they come crop up.

Recently I read about a smart move by a MacDonald's outlet in Paris, France or so…
It gladdened my heart. This outlet actually went beyond the standard offerings expected of an average McDonald's. The customers love them more for the additional initiatives. You must plan to do more to ensure continuous patronage by clients.

And for those who choose to be a franchisor, if this model is part of your long term plan of setting up your enterprise, start documenting as you build your successful system that can be replicated elsewhere. A tested business formula that has become a profit generator. And that is equally cool, if the laws of your country will effectively back you up against copyright infringement.

Working Capital

Have some money kept aside to take care of the daily needs of the business, is a must. Also, there are unexpected occasions when some opportunities such as discounted items could come your way. There will also be times when you cannot rule out to take care of some emergencies.

At the onset of your business, there is always a struggle of having extra cash. Different competing commitments would come up, yet the business bills must be paid.
Try to estimate the total amount of working capital and keep it in the bank or have part of it with you in the office.

See the link to my free video course on working Capital and Cash-flow Management at the last pages...

It is very important to determine the amount of money you will need to start and manage the business in the short term. Six to nine months is a good projection. However, it all depends on your industry. Monthly working capital or whatever period that augurs well with your business must be worked out. You need to be fluid. It is a balancing act because you don't have to keep too much idle funds around.
You may not have all the money at onset. The trick is you may need to borrow some amount from friends, loved ones and other sources. But you must envisage from your projections how you will want to pay back.

Personally speaking, way back in 1994, I had a cause to sell my car to complete a loan given by a group of different individuals when I wanted to start my eye clinic. I had already calculated that, if the sales did not come as expected, that would be the asset to be liquefied (turned to cash). I was mentally ready to go through the inconvenience of not having a car before it became a reality - six months after - much as I worked hard to prevent that.

Your Industry's Admission Score

There is an amount of capital that you need to give the minimum-viable-product (MVP) in the eyes of your market niche. Otherwise you will have to wait until you get this amount of money.

Different industries demand certain minimum-viable-product as accepted in the eyes of target consumers.

What I mean by a "**minimum-viable-product or service**" is the minimum content acceptable by an average consumer. Liken it to the minimum entry point for a school admission.

This is very important where there are other competitors who have been providing same services. You do not want to go too low in the eyes of consumers about what you want to offer. This is not to say you cannot take it a step higher than what prevails in your industry.

But it is good to test the basics and you may step up over time. That gives room for experimentation and accurate products, from the feedbacks you get from discerning consumers.

Therefore, identify this minimum before you come out or you wait until you have the money to produce such a total and complete package.

Home-Based And Alternatives

Can you work from home within the legal requirements of your locale and industry? Do you have the personal discipline to have a home-based business? You will know…

Find out and start something. Otherwise, you may need to share space elsewhere. At the extreme, we have heard of people using their vehicle as the first office space.

And if you desire to go the way of an internet based business, go ahead as long as paying clients can be attracted to your website. But be conversant with its rules of engagement on this channel of doing business. If you can't afford a paying website, start with a free website. Later on, you can re-launch your own domain name with time with your own webpages. But this is not really an expensive undertaking.

Acquiring Your Tools

If you can lease some equipment, then go ahead and pay back in bits since you may not have the capital for outright purchase to start with. To augment my starting capital, I took my dining chairs from home, to use as part of the initial furniture of my front office, back in 1994. Though a few months later, I was able to replace them with more appropriate furniture. I took them back home. *With my younger family, we used to eat on our laps while sitting on the sofa.*

To get basic furniture and equipment, I deposited some money and invited the suppliers to come to my office to authenticate my business. Most of them got some deposits and released the items.

And I was able to pay the remainder over a few months.

This is where your interpersonal relationship and integrity must come into play.

It can speed up your inertia, save you money and help with financing the business. All these creative thoughts, you must come up with, where feasible, so that you can get some equipment in place in the absence of inadequate capital.

Financing Without Money

As I have earlier mentioned, when starting out a new venture, you may choose to approach some suppliers of the resources you would need. You would encourage him or her to visit your business space. This is a good tactic, to convince them of your seriousness. If you are lucky, that could trigger some trust and attract some waivers, so that you can start in earnest despite limited funds.

As you know, every supplier is desirous of increased patronage, in their own competitive industry. Such a supplier may modify their terms when dealing with an honest and convincing buyer. Successful business interactions are essentially based on trust, between suppliers and buyers. You are the buyer in this scenario.

In the presence of unlimited funds, do not be carried away by the share amount of it. Do not spend everything even if you could.
Use only the minimum amount that is permissible for a successful start. All new businesses have their respective inertia before they reach the cruising speed, irrespective of the capital sunk in.
There-after, you can test and measure the returns on the funds you have expended so far. Be aware that too much funds may stifle the creativity of the business owner and his team. The superfluous funding can make the brain go lazy.

It is true that inadequate capital can delay a business from starting or even stifle growth; we should squeeze everything we can from every cent. Additional funds can be added in time and when necessary.

Some businesses can start and do well without the popular formal business plan. You can get your feet wet and make adjustments, as you steer the business through its life cycle of infancy, adolescence before you get to the maturity phase.
The practical steps to go about this, you can filter out from this book.

'MUYIWA OSIFUYE

Nearly all business plans contain sections that deal with income, expenditure and projected profit; these are arrived at, based on certain parameters of the strategic plan of the founders.

The Business Plan Mystery

On your own, you can easily draw up a single-page business plan. That may suffice, even though truly, elsewhere it could be a document of many pages, especially if such a company is talking to creditors and prospective investors.

The secret is that these people look beyond your business plan! *It is about you or your team; what you are made of.* Your lender or banker won't let you know this. It goes beyond your business plan on paper. It is just a plan any statistician can draw up.
What do they look at in addition?
It is the hunger inside of you, your capability, the ruggedness and smartness when you are being interviewed - and your self-esteem.

So let us go back to the financials.
You will estimate how many clients are expected to buy from you and the price they would easily pay; this is your sales revenue.

Your estimated total revenue in a month is not your cash profit. You must deduct your direct spending - that have to do with sales - from this figure. The direct spending is known as cost-of-goods sold. Get a good part-time accounting professional.
Having done so, what remains is the gross profit, which is still different from the net profit or net income. There will be other contingent expenditures determined by your situation, this will be deducted again and what is left may be a net loss or net profit for that month.

Yes, some spending could result in a loss, especially if there is a need for

The Small Business Starter's Guide

a quick cash commitment while the sales are not high enough initially. This is not unusual for some new businesses. But in subsequent weeks or months, you may see profit in your cash flow. Since cash is king, respect it more than the receivables - which you could have given out on credit.

Before you launch your business, if you are a sole business owner, set aside money that can take care of your own personal wellbeing, at least for the first six months or more.
Your business projection, either written as a formal business plan or not, should be regarded as simply a forecast. The risk of disappointment is there.
Even if your business posts profits immediately, it is an opportunity to take a portion of the cash and inject it into the business to increase patronage.
If you ask a mentor or a consultant for some tips or you have done your thorough research, you must still avail yourself of the rudimentary knowledge, about your business to make it more profitable.

Businesses are meant to grow. Nobody expects your business to start from maturity with a Big Bang. Go through a natural growth process. Growth would be expedited in the presence of strong marketing skills, adequate working capital with unique message and solutions as strongly desired by your target market.

In every industry, there is a minimum accepted perception of professionalism and seriousness by prospective customers. If you lack the minimum capital to set up your business up to that level, I will strongly advise that you wait, until you have the minimum resources or outlook. I repeat that again. Don't waste the resources you have now.

If you rush ahead, you would have tied down the little resources made available. The low patronage that ensues, would lead to frustration and self-blame. You might think it was a bad business idea. So choose your industry very well, with regards to the capital at your disposal.

Some industries may surprisingly need a minimum capital of small funds and the players are good to go. In some others industries, a larger capital would be too small to make any basic impact. It is like having an airline business with a single aircraft. How far can you compete? You may augment for shortage of cash with a credit line or leasing of assets, if you are sure of your projected income, associated risks peculiar to the business and costs.

To get going seriously speaking, some people have used resources at hand, such as their cars, as a store and office where the goods can be stored. The creative alternatives are always thrown up when cash is limited. I just told you about borrowing my dining-chairs from home for my office, for about six months.

Business planning projections are better made, if one approaches them with a balanced outlook, devoid of too much optimism. It is less risky even if all facts point to the contrary. It is better to be pleasantly surprised than drawing too rosy a projection.

Things tend to be different in the trenches. I can tell you that from my 30 years of insight into studying and being involved in small enterprise management. I am an unrepentant optimist who also believes in the unpredictable nature of *earthquakes and spewing of volcanoes,* figuratively speaking.

You don't want to be seriously discouraged in midstream. You don't want to have sleepless nights that no sedative pills can cure. You want to be healthy even if the first two months post a loss.

You will investigate and work on it. You can't be squeamish. As an entrepreneur you can't be too apologetic, when making vital decisions, especially financial matters.

A few years back, I recall when I tried to diversify into another line of business. This idea eventually collapsed because my staff messed the business up. The luck I had was that the money invested was a portion out of reserve. Even though I lost part of that investment but my primary business still thrived on.
The lesson learnt here is that in every business, especially the small ones - even during the teething period – you must stash something away and nothing is too small. My reserve reduced my agony. It is important to have an entrenched savings culture in the organization.

However, please do not unnecessarily save or cut costs, at the detriment of quality service and compromised processes. It is a balancing act.
Do not be penny wise, pound foolish. Right? That act of financial discipline, I must admit is very tough, but one must not give up.
To put aside a small fraction of your profit is never too much. The accumulated reserve gives you and the business peace of mind. Another advantage is that in due course, a portion of this money can be utilized to try out other investments, to see possibility of attractive returns.
The additional venture doesn't have to be big. Whatever the accumulated gains, are simply returned into the reserve or used to pursue other opportunities.

Pains Of Financing
You can also pool funds from friends, kith and kin. This might not be possible in some cases. I have not been very lucky in this direction.
The much capital I needed to start my eye clinic in 1994 was through s close in-law, who stood in as a guarantor to the consortium of individual lenders. And the rates were at *shylock* interest rates. I knew the excruciating terms before I took these monies. But I concluded it was better to birth the business into reality, after years of carrying the idea in my mind, due to lack of capital.

°MUYIWA OSIFUYE

I knew if I couldn't meet up with the time of full repayment, I had an asset I could sell to complete my loan, to save face and maintain my dignity. Good to say, most of these objectives were met.

The business came into existence. And I was happy that I could earn my own income and I was financially independent. As I have said before; towards the tail end - sixth month - of servicing my loan balance, the business slowed down. I had my plan B, which I knew, even before I took the facility. I simply sold my jalopy car, used the total money to pay a particular lender his balance. No extra cash remained with me that month, after paying some overhead, including my small staff salaries. But I was happy and proud of myself; I had started my own business! Since then, it has been a roller-coaster in my world of entrepreneurship; challenging, tough but interesting. It has been knocks on the head and applause for victories won – a mishmash of reality.

The next thing I did was to look beyond this cubicle of a clinic, which was what I could afford to start with. I decided on a bigger space, at a more befitting location in another part of town. This would take another clinic sharing same premises with a photo studio, with a separate layout.

So savings from the modest income was started in earnest after liquidating the initial loan. As you would expect, I personally sacrificed a lot of things. I skipped lunches amongst other things, at this helluva of a time, to meet my renewed set objectives.

It took me three months to put the second office right before opening to the public in 1997. Much was still done, to get the place up to taste, with recycled funds from the business. I did not want to borrow at a high cost, so it took some time - about a year - to get the place to my taste.

At this second location, I eventually stayed for over twelve years, before a need to relocate elsewhere. Hopefully as I write this, we will re-launch and have a few of my ventures under one roof.

For those who wish to borrow money to do your business, I will not discourage you. There are many obvious reasons of using *"other people's money"* OPM, to invest in business.

For instance, if you are into trading and you have customers waiting to be sold to; and all parameters of the exchange and transactions are known thoroughly by you, but for working capital or needed resources, do go ahead and raise the money.

Do your cost-benefit analysis, ok?
This means that you know your cost; you know your selling price. If the terms of the financing, that is, the interest rate and other costs are much less than your total sales, then go for the credit facility. You cannot borrow the principal with the attendant interests (the cost of funds) and you are expected to pay back in three months, when you know your business will not make profitable returns until after four, five months or much later. That is mismatching.

Some businesses - please do note this - within certain circumstances would find it beneficial to take a credit facility. Some may not be favourably disposed. Study your circumstances well or get a good business consultant, to assist you in arriving at an effective decision.

Your matching has to be balanced. Financial obligations that go out ought to be taken care of with expected cash income and the cash in your coffers, within a period.

Cash flow management needs proper matching in all businesses especially in small businesses. Cash is king; don't be fooled by your huge profit on your balance sheet, which is on paper. Do you have most of that same figure in your bank?

In subsequent paragraphs, I will talk more on this delicate issue that could make a business go down, if not well attended to. And it is easy to do, because it is almost akin to our personal spending decisions. Surprisingly, many chief executives do not transfer this safe spending behaviour to running their enterprises.

Cash-flow: The Life Line

I am not turning you to an auditor, an accountant or a tax consultant in this book. But you need to have a basic idea about some financial matters, when it comes to money, cost and profits. Engage the services of an accountant to guide you through the life cycle of your business. But the little snippet I will share here will make you appreciate what your account manager talks about. With what I will highlight here, you can even contribute and dialogue much better, when you meet with those professionals.

It simply means determining how much cash you are very sure comes in and goes out of the business.

This is subject to the trade credits you give out and to the financial obligations the business must pay, within a time frame.

When there is a mismatch, indiscipline or over optimism in the management of your cash flow, your business may eventually perish right there, before your eyes.

Your huge fixed assets may not save you in most cases.

Why?

Because theses fixed assets like tools, equipment, furniture, buildings and so on, may not easily be converted to cash, when needed urgently.

As cash serves as the life blood, that every business needs to circulate through its system; so manage your cash-flow very well. There is always a simple way to go about it. However, you can make your business to become a much capitalized one. You make it stronger as you return the

trickles of cash back into the system. This act of financial expediency could keep you away from creditors, where necessary.
Within six weeks of your starting, you should have an idea of some recurring basic expenditures and projected income.
Without proper planning and management of cash, that goes in and out, a business may just be on its way to financial suffocation and lost opportunities.

Proper cash management is the life blood of any business. It is readily the means of exchange. It is the heart of an enterprise, irrespective if it was setup as a profit or a non-profit venture. As a matter of fact, all non-profits need cash to survive too, how much more, a profit oriented business like yours.

Whether your business deals in little cents or billions of Dollars, Naira (as we spend in Nigeria), Euro, Pounds or any currency, the same mechanism applies. In the absence of proper cash flow management, a billion dollar business may suffer and die. On the other hand, a little enterprise of few cents, with well managed cash flow, would at its own level of well-oiled operation, continues to be fruitful.
Though the bigger organizations and their big figures would need more painstaking attention, that is not to say, some managers of big companies won't frown at a loss of a small amount of money.

Therefore, the basic cash management concept rests on balancing your inflow and outflow. You may not be an accountant, but every smart man or woman in her personal life monitors how much cash goes in and out. We do this routinely, so that we don't find ourselves in the red.
But truly due to circumstances beyond our control - on a personal note - we do at times, find ourselves in the red. Same could happen to a business. So as a smart person, you ensure your cash balance is positive within a time frame. If you have done so successfully in your personal life, then simply extend the mindset to the business.

°MUYIWA OSIFUYE

Since a business has a life of its own and it uses cash at hand as its oxygen, therefore you watch for its depletion and replenishment, always.

Cash movement involves:
knowing the money that comes in,
the one we think will come in and
the amount that we want to spend, within a time period.
One needs to balance this tripod very well.

There is a little concept in managing funds or cash flow in business, which is called matching.
It basically means you can only spend the cash you have received. This leaves you with a zero cash balance. A state of neither credit nor debt. But if a serious need for cash rears up its head, immediately after this zero balance, and you must meet this newer obligation, then you have to look for cash somehow.

Your expected monetary sales – your receivables- cannot be of help at that moment. You may reach out to borrow money or sell an asset for cash, without delay to meet up. Do note, it takes time to sell some assets to receive cash. And this can be frustrating.

(By the way, in your asset portfolio, use your extra funds to buy into easily convertible assets and fixed assets. They all have their advantages. The fixed assets tend to give higher returns, when disposed of, but they don't sell fast enough).

So how do you manage a good cash flow movement? In addition to my earlier description, you will look at some factors. You will use the following factors such as time, credit, debit, receivables and payables. This will also include personality or integrity of the company in the eyes of suppliers, findings in the internal records, risk assessment and a strong intuition to manage cash flow. To ensure you have some cash reserve, you don't need to spend everything in your coffer.

You may plead for time with those that expect cash from your business, be it internally or externally. Your integrity or organization's goodwill – a valuable asset - by third parties could allow for a good credit, when you run out of resources.
This money you owe is the payable. Your sales history gives you an idea of the maximum you can owe, within a time frame.

Be aware of how much cash and receivables, will come your company's way, within a time frame. The time duration you give credit to your own buyers, must not disrupt your own cash at hand.
Likewise, match your own promise of when to pay your creditors. Keep your word. You will need it in the future. You never can tell.
Don't keep away from your creditor or lender. Always reach across to him or her. Don't be ashamed to dialogue with him and be sorry later

Time and cash to be paid can also be stretched out. You ensure the business is with adequate cash reserve, despite carrying out its financial obligations. In the same vein, that decision should ensure the suppliers or those who expect cash from the business including staff salaries, emoluments and overhead can be spread out.

Risk management comes in by looking at the different sections of the business. This includes cash-flow management, to look at where things could go wrong. Therefore adjustments must be made as needed, in an objective manner without any sentiment. Intuition comes into play if there is a conviction of earlier success in making decisions about cash. In this case, a forecast can be made about money that could come in or be expended. This approach is not for everybody; therefore, the findings from the company's records and the risk testing must be utilized. In managing cash flow, a mixture of part payment in cash with debit or credit is undertaken, depending on whether you are the buyer or the seller.

Before I depart from here, can we appreciate that what is written on the invoice or receipted is your sales. This is not your profit. Other direct costs will have to be deducted, to arrive at the profit per unit item sold. Some entrepreneurs mix up these concepts.

Don't give too much credit facility because it can affect your cash flow. Your receivables may not be translated to cash, as expected. The bird in hand at times, is worth two in the bush. You may have receivables that never get paid for. Keep greed out of it

In those countries where business litigation is difficult, avoid giving out too much credit. Many buyers would choose to default and you expend more money pursuing your money.

Some people relish seeing their sales books show so much receivable, yet their debtors don't pay them on time. Piling up, the figure is not cash in your coffer.

Don't be greedy too, to take so much on credit, given by a sweet talking supplier. Be suspicious when suppliers want to dump their unsold inventories on your business, and later on nag you to pay up.

Cash management is a discipline in terms of commitment to a project that your cash-flow can support. You can't expect 20,000 units of your currency as profit by the third month and venture into an undertaken of 90,000 at once. This is a mismatch as other routine activities and financial commitments will suffer.

You will wait till you have the financial muscle that could absorb the higher figure. Being overzealous, being over optimistic and naïve in business operations and business management can create a cash flow problem. Some people allow their ego to push them into bankruptcy. They want to do the volume of business like a big competitor. They are in a hurry to employ certain number of staff or are inpatient in scaling the business, to give the semblance of successful enterprise.

If you have to do this, it must be done with caution. It doesn't take long before a weak foundation crumbles. In managing your cash-flow, you will need to juggle different elements of your costs. As your customers owe you, which are receivables, your business must also manage your payables, which is money you owe your own suppliers.

Consider this; your accounting books may show a higher profit, while the cash in the bank is much less, because of much credit given out which is not yet paid. Your company may owe too.
Use the robust cash you have in your account to service your indebtedness. You must have a good business model and cash strategy to manage your cash-flow.
Try to avoid a mismatch in your cash flow which might creep in within a period, like quarterly or half-yearly at most. External factors beyond your control may bring up problems to an enterprise. Deal with it with creativity.
You may need to go out to augment by borrowing either cash or other non-cash resources to keep the business running, to save face.
I had had a cause to borrow money on my personal effort, outside the income from the business, to supplement salaries. But I had to find a way out to prevent a reoccurrence.

At times, downsizing might be the solution. Even if you are the sole employee, you may choose to "downsize" your lifestyle. It is either you get rid of that expensive car, getting a smaller office, stopping that annual vacation, so as to create a smooth cash-flow in the process.
Proper cash-flow management is a sensitive aspect of any enterprise, irrespective of its profitability or profit potential.
It demands discipline, foresight, proper understanding of the internal aspects of your business and the external aspects of the locality and environment your business is.

°MUYIWA OSIFUYE

Expenses Aren't The Same
A word of caution!
There may be variations of the general idea I will be explaining here. Some expenses are somehow difficult to categorize.
Accounting conventions in some states, countries or industries may be slightly different from the simple approaches I have am going to give. Your accountant must still be approached for further guidance.

So let's proceed.

The costing technique makes it easier for business owners and accountants to monitor the best way to run the finances of the company. It gives a clearer picture of the functions of the different expenditures, we make and how to get the best out of them.
It gives us the opportunity to maximize and optimize the use of money.

They are also essential, when preparing both financial and tax returns, for the regulatory bodies. They give us a clear picture of the costing structure of our business, because a well-managed cost management or expenditure can result in higher profits.
Cost management ensures discipline and guides you on where certain expenditures can be adjusted, without compromising the quality of the current service. Good costing structure or layout helps in achieving a robust and strong balance sheet.

I will explain types of costs without going deeply into the realm where accountants can do justice to the nitty-gritty. However, as a business owner or chief executive, you need to have some basic knowledge.

The direct cost is an expenditure that is directly related to the product that is being sold to the market place. If I were a butcher, my direct cost is the cost of the mutton or sheep as I bought it from the farm.

The indirect costs may include the rent of my butcher's shop, salaries, utilities charges and other overheads. The indirect cost in this business will also comprise, the transportation cost to the farm and other attendant costs that ensure the sheep is made ready to be butchered for sale.

A direct cost or indirect cost may contain two other components namely, fixed and variable costs. That is, a direct cost can be subdivided into fixed or variable cost.
The indirect cost can also be subdivided into fixed and variable cost.

Fixed Cost is the compulsory expenditure that must be made, whether there is any activity in the business or not. For instance, the butcher must pay the rent, salaries, some utilities and do more, irrespective of whether he makes the sales or not.

The pieces of furniture, the cooling freezers, motorized cutting saws and all the tools of the trade are all fixed costs.
(However, these particular examples given are further categorized as fixed assets, when drawing up the balance sheet of the company. Because they are tangible and not easily perishable items, as they last over a period of time).

If you bought a jet bombardier or Gulf Stream that would be a fixed cost. But if you hire one when you need it, then the expenditure is a variable cost. You pay according to the frequency of your usage.

Variable cost is that expenditure that goes strictly in tandem, with the level of business activity. The amount of variable costs is influenced by the frequency or turnover of the activities in that business.

If the butcher expands his business, and he employs more hands which goes with additional salaries, this particular variable cost has increased.

°MUYIWA OSIFUYE

If he feels a gadget can give him better returns and therefore downsizes, he has less staff, the variable cost, goes down. If he discovers it's cheaper to buy his sheep by joining a cooperative of other butchers, his procurement expenditure goes down, so his variable cost.

Let's quickly look at how the costs of fixed assets are used in profit calculation. If you buy equipment, you can't deduct its purchased price for that same month, when preparing your books. The tagged price is divided across a pre-determined months or years and a figure is allocated to each month.

Loosely, this is the way fixed assets are financially treated, because they are used into the future. Such an item may be physical or intangible like software applications; their usefulness covers many financial periods or years. You determine the total number of years you think, its utility values would have been squeezed out of the asset.
There are different accounting methods of calculating depreciation of assets, over time.

Let's assume it is five years, lets us use one accounting convention, the flat rate method – not compensating for inflation.
To determine what will be the allocated cost for the monthly usage. Divide the cost of the asset by sixty months, which is five years.
Note that the item may be disposed of at the end of the fifth year, at the value the market dictates, the so-called residual value.
Let's leave that for now.

This monthly figure, which is a fixed cost, is added to the other monthly expenditures. I will stop here; an accountant knows how to address different fixed costs of different items. But what I have done is to open your eyes to these costs.

Different Shades Of Profit

You can know the monthly figures meant for salaries, rents and other overheads. So you add all the costs that make up the fixed costs with the variable costs for the month and that gives the total costs.

Your insurance, legal and government obligations would fall into different categories of cost schedule as I have stated earlier. Your accountant will guide with regards to your industry and your location of business. After the removal of the fixed costs and the variable cost from the total sales in a particular month, what is left is regarded as the Gross profit.
The popular deduction you remove yet again after gross profit is tax. It is after this the real profit is arrived. This net profit may all be in cash or partially in cash.
The outstanding profit is the receivables - the sales on credit or delayed payment from clients within that month.

For yearly financial report of your business, your accountant may give you an overall profitability of your business, as EBITDA.
This acronym is from the **E**arnings, **B**efore, **I**nterest, **D**epreciation and **A**mortization. Each subsequent item is deducted from the earnings which is the gross profit after sales.
The figure so calculated and arrived at is the real profit. The EBITDA.

In a particular year, you may not have the Depreciation, Amortization and even Tax (if your business is on a tax exemption holiday).
So you will simply have an EBIT as the net profit, without Depreciation and Amortization. Earning is your gross profit.
Interest is the amount your business is paying on a loan or drawn overdraft.
Depreciation is the cost you have allocated due to the usage of a fixed asset. Over time, you assume, the asset has been depleted of all the juice,

the utility value. Thereafter, depreciation over time becomes zero. The sucked orange is ready to be thrown away.
However some depleted assets can be refurbished. I guess accountants will tell us how to put this back in the books, since I am not one.

Amortization is the amount of money you put aside, in paying for an asset that is directly linked to the business. It could be the periodical money you pay before taking full ownership of an asset, essentially, major equipment.

Be Smart; Keep The Records
You must know how to do basic stock taking and book keeping. This must be prepared before the arrival of your accountant, who possibly you may invite weekly, to complete your books. When I started my business this was what I did, 9 months down the line, when I was buoyant enough, to pay a visiting accountant.

If you don't know the financial status of your business, even if it's still located on your dining table, then you are doing injustice to your business. Your business is simply groping in the dark. You will never it's worth and financial state.
So get your daily entries done. It is not difficult. A well designed and regular record keeping, helps to keep track of the essential and relevant activities in managing a business.
If you don't keep records, you are just groping in the dark. You can't keep the business.

What needs to be recorded will include relevant activities, inputs and outputs that constitute a business system. They will include items that have to do with financial transactions, inventory of goods and services, processing of customers (complimentary or not), the staff and other external activities that can affect the business.

The advantages are numerous, such records minimize pilferage, they assist in risk management, and they give insight into many aspects of the business. If well designed and analysed, they reveal so much that a business can work with for success.

Record keeping of your finance and accounting, are important. They matter. It makes it easy to prepare your tax returns, without cheating yourself and government. Let your accountant professional come in here to do it better.

Apart from the physical documentation, today, there are many software and application tools, for different industries, that can be sourced online. You can also commission a software developer to design your own unique tools for various types of record keeping. Some may be free, usable for common activities but not tailored to all businesses.

Auditing covers financial and the inventory of items. Cash audit and other inventories are the most important.
Depending on the size of the company, tools, equipment, others assets including personnel auditing are done periodically.
If you ran a restaurant, weekly auditing would be necessary of food stuff and other relevant items. And it could be done on a monthly or yearly basis subject to the type of business.
It is good to tabulate these figures. It could be done on computer, using the spread sheet application of your choice.

Auditing is part of the control system. It allows you to know what is coming in and going out. It discourages pilfering and encourages optimization of resources, whether cash or the bags of cinnamon kept in the store of your eatery. It lets you know when to place an order for your bulk stationery, assuming yours is a legal firm. From past auditing, then you can buy in bulk at a discount. It saves time and money.

'MUYIWA OSIFUYE

There are many auditing applications out there, some free and some modestly priced. For financial movements, it is better done in-house monthly. I will advise your accountant comes in weekly, to work on your postings. Thereafter, financial statements are prepared monthly. This was how I started as a one-man army, many years back.

It is about respecting the business. He would have given you or the relevant staff, basic training on how to keep simple records for his later use. You will need the services of an accounts professional that knows about your industry. Big or small, it is wise an enterprise keeps its books.

Good book keeping will reveal your financial reality of sales, actual profit or loss and expenditures. Many businesses owners tend to mix them up. And they get excited with the cash in their drawers, which they spend whenever they are excited.
Your accountant will prepare your cash statements and also your balance sheet, whether it is a one man show or bigger business.
He will tell you the basic indices you should watch out for, about the business.

Your banks might need to see your books when you choose to approach them, for a loan facility. Opportunities do come but for lack of capital. An overdraft can go a long way, to raise money; a lender would give, if your books are well prepared.

Take Cash, Not Profit
Let me quickly share this popular school of thought, on how to increase profit. It rests on these tactics: Do what you can, to increase the number of new customers – you may give incentives for referrals.
Increase the unit of sales or increase your price - you may introduce your offerings as bundles or combos. Your outfit may also do something to increase the frequency of purchase.

And how do you do that? Provide newer versions of your service or run a promo for a limited period of time.

You may get a significant discount from another company, that offers other products or services that your clients would need. Strike the bargain on their behalf and share the profit with the other company. In other words, look at each situation and device possibilities.

Let us look at the basic ways of generating income in a typical business and these thoughts I will explain here will be seen in most businesses. If you have a product either made by your business or bought from a supplier, you can sell such at a margin. When you deduct some relevant costs, you now have a net profit. So that is a basic retailing method. However, do realize that, if you don't have exclusive access to this product to sell, other competitors would appear. If there is nothing unique to all the participants, then profitability is negatively affected, as you will all compete on the basis of price reduction over time.

If by all means you must sell these products for reasons best known to you, I will advise you look for supplementary products or service to add. You will sell as a combo but pick a supplementary product or service that is difficult to come by, by your competitors.
By virtue of size, big companies are slow to react to such a tactic, when small companies offer similar products.

Give a better user experience. Make your profit quickly before the big company unleashes its financial power. If you carry out your marketing, using the guerrilla style, it is slow and challenging but your business is not easily exposed to docile competitors.
Before they realize what is amiss, you have taken a chunk of the market. But at this point, do think big, take the next step of getting bigger, to scale your business. It is a choice though.

I have a personal story to share, that since the beginning of 2015,
I discovered a veritable platform to sell a highly competitive product. The strategy I have chosen after successful test marketing is to find a way of reaching more buyers, through some quiet channels.

Using the traditional advertising would bring in huge competition, from those with bigger capital. This will reduce my profit seriously.
If the product is produced by you and it is relatively difficult to copy then, you can do well in that business, if the consumers really yearn for it.

You can easily device means of making more profit. The secret; if practicable, take the unconventional route from the popular, to reach your target market.
That reminds me of an unemployed architect, who took a kiosk space and offered quality consultancy at one dollar at a market fair.
That was his ingenious but humble stepping stone in the midst of lack and noise of the big firms. Today, he rakes in his modest millions.

This is a testimonial, to submit that innovative thoughts could skyrocket us to our goals, be it money or otherwise. Thinking differently and understanding human psychology, to work around their circumspection.

Surviving Recession

A business owner must be an all involving personality; making moves most of the time and not waiting until something ruffles the feather of the business.
Running a business is about taking a leadership role.
A business leader must be aware of the whims and caprices of the market place.
Even in times of economic depression, your business must find out the new need of the market. You will find them at the lower rung of the hierarchy of needs - the basics needed by Man for survival.

And believe you me, they are always there for to you discover, if you are not so rigid, in your thinking. By so doing, you will make your profit, it may not be much, but your business will be able to ride through the tempestuous wave.

And when things get better, the business strategy can be readjusted, to tap into new opportunities.
Cash is king during recession. I won't get tired of saying this. I missed the importance of cash in my earlier years of business for huge projected profit. To ensure profitability, you have to be creative about managing your cost, without compromising the quality of your service too much. At periods of this uncertainty, the untouched savings come in handy. Suddenly more opportunities are available with less competition, then go after them. You can tone down the service, stripping down the product, to the basic essentials.
Reduce price and people are ready to pay. Business ideas that flourish are those consumptions that people cannot but spend money on.

Other Side-Incomes
Being a partaker of the profit of another company is a good way of making passive income, from investing in stocks and shares, as well as in monetary and capital market instruments.
They come in various names and descriptions. Let an expert explain their nuances to you. Meanwhile only use a portion (30% in total) of your profit in those markets.

As a beginner, only invest the money you can afford to lose, in the stock or finance market. It is a form of passive income outside your control. Build a business instead to generate the income you have control over.

If you are a part owner of an enterprise, periodical dividends is another way of making money. Your capital contribution to the ownership of an enterprise through different arrangements, agreeable in options or purchased shares, makes you a partaker in the financial fortunes of that enterprise.

So when profit is declared, you will be given your commensurate amount. Likewise if there is a loss or no declaration of dividend, you are exposed to same. Such enterprises could be private or publicly listed. Beyond the expected dividend pay outs, the value of you units or shares you paid for might go higher or lower over a period of time.

You may need in addition to your observation, a professional stock brokerage firm or broker that can guide you. But don't put absolute trust in them. Do your own due diligence.

Trading in stocks, shares and other commercial papers (instruments) comes with its own inherent risk and returns, if you choose this route to earn an income, rather than starting a physical enterprise of your own. But this route cannot be coined as a business but as a financial more-risky-investment route.

The companies involved could be small start-ups or big corporations as listed on the major stock exchanges. The choice is yours for your company to buy into as a form of diversification of cash from your business. Another stream of income, which if you are not sure.

However, a note of warning; a non-investment - with the idle cash intact in the kitty- might be a better choice, until the signs are convincing to put your cash in any other investment.

How To Tame Business Risks?

Nearly all attempts we make in life and business are projected in our minds to bring about a preconceived expectation. The outcome is all a probability. We may hit the target and we may not. That is our reality. Therefore every activity, every decision that takes place in an enterprise carries the risk factor. The relative strength of risks is subject to peculiar circumstances.

The essence of having a risk management policy in place – irrespective of the size of any enterprise – is to eliminate failures or at least, ameliorate whatever challenges that might arise.

It will be foolhardy; to just take things for granted or pretend things will sort themselves out for good. In business or personal life, this mindset can be likened to gambling since you are not too sure of the outcome.

Risk management involves both the internal and external factors that can influence a business. Such a policy may be simple or robust in nature, depending on the complexity of the enterprise and the industry.

Now, how do you go about putting up a risk control mechanism? Identify the major sensitive areas in all ramifications. For example, examine what could affect profitability, cost and the continued existence of the business. You carry out this exercise, both on the internal and external environments of the business.

The main thrust of the mechanism, so designed, must identify all the possible risks, measure them and establish solution pathways to ameliorate or avoid them.
And there must be an on-going appraisal of the mechanism, since circumstances change in business.

I will just give a simple illustration, using the human resources challenge, common to all businesses. Beyond this you can derive the possibilities of risky points in your business.
Do you have only one staff manning a very important aspect of the business, such that in his or her absence, the business comes to a stop and a loss is made?
Do you have a plan in place, where you can quickly get a temporary skilled staff, while you run another interview process?
Have you been keeping money aside, to hire a second staff, so that, that

aspect of business won't be left in the cold?
What is the opportunity cost of this redundant staff when compared to possible loss of business, if a highly skilled worker suddenly resigns?

Let's look at another example of an expected sales projection within a time frame. Imagine if there is a shortfall in the projected amount of patronage and sales, say, in a month; what are the plans designed to ameliorate this shortfall?
What are the plans to prevent this?

Externally, most factors that affect a business are beyond the control of the managers. But that would not make you to fold your arms. The way to navigate through is to think through the possibilities of what might go wrong. Afterwards you design a set of activities to avoid them, should they occur, so that the business will not be battered too badly. Get an expert to help you do this, possibly risk managers and other experts in the insurance field, doing it with an honest mind and not to promote his or her product.

As a matter of fact, the conglomerates do a lot of lobbying in the corridors of power, to influence policies that might work against their businesses. It is a way of reducing their risk exposure to unfavourable government policies. They have to leave their comfort zone to do this.

At their own humble corner, small business owners should strive to be in control of the input that can affect their business. If the resources are not available at the early stage of the business, it is important they work towards being in control.

For example, if you have only one supplier of a very important item that goes into your production, the business is at the mercy of that supplier. You must put up a mechanism to minimize your dependence or eliminate that threat. The actions to take will depend on the circumstance of your business.

Crowding To Fund
I will need to touch on this new interest in the world of financing. I chose not to add it earlier on, under sources of financing. The model is somehow new today. But I believe it stems from the traditional cooperative and social media culture in quick enterprise building.

Crowd funding is a new way to source for finance. It has become popular, of late, in project funding. It has leveraged on today's technology through the Internet platform to pool funds across to execute a project.

Contributors are promised a predetermined reward, after the project has come on stream. There are different modalities of participation and distribution of rewards or dividends to the contributors. This new phenomenon attracts participants across the world, who may not necessarily share same sentiments with the sponsor of the project. Within a designated time frame, the funds are quickly raised through a reputable website.

I am yet to study this new development of its attendant risks and rewards, as we approach the future in its business application and development.

But it looks good, based on trust with share of manageable risk. However, modified versions of this concept are done offline, by some entrepreneurs who could pull some people together and convince others of her project.
What makes it attractive online is that, you only ask for a little money, contributed by thousands or millions. So the huge sum can be raised within a short time frame.

°MUYIWA OSIFUYE

Twists About M&A

Mergers and Acquisitions even though tend to be written together, but I will give a simple explanation of what each terminology means.

A merger takes place when two of equal strength businesses decide to become one new entity. That is, each can derive certain advantages from the other, while by so doing, their weakness are diminished.
The union is expected to evolve into a singular but solid company, with a new distinct identity.
One company does not buy over the other company. It is a mutual agreement of dissolving to a new but seemingly singular identity, which must be done in accordance of the laws of a state, country and global business practice.

There are challenges in terms of organizational structure, the feelings of the workforce and control of the executive powers of the new identity. These and more must be well discussed before concluding on the merger. The full assimilation may take up to a year.

At times, as we have known, the deal may sail through or have hiccups even after the merging. There is also the naughty issue about the false financial picture given to the public, with claims that the two participants are of equal strength. This may not be true in some cases.

A monopolistic behemoth – the giant company that controls almost the market - could arise in the market place after the marriage, debarring other lowly players from competing. Mergers are neither here nor there. Quite complicated but it is a useful concept in many aspects of the business world.

Acquisition on the other hand, is where a supposedly stronger company buys out a target company. The name of the target tends to be retired, finally. A more advantaged company approaches, to buy a "lesser" endowed company. It could also play out, that a company approaches another relatively bigger company offering itself for purchase.

The company that is bought is called a target. Some entrepreneurs have capitalized on this arrangement- metaphorically and literally speaking – by giving up their enterprise, to be acquired.
The resulting cash, they collect could be used to start another business or used as they deem fit. Some may still ask for a bit of the equity in the merged organization, while they take less pay out and remain on the board.

There is less problem of assimilation in acquisition, - such as culture - since definitely, one company has the bigger financial muscle and the other has decided to relinquish its ownership and control. Full absorption may take place within a year.

Acquisition is a very powerful idea to leapfrog your financial base quickly. If you envision a strong capability to make huge growth happen than the organic growth of your primary business, then go for it.
You may even take the business public after the acquisition to increase the value of the new company. You will need good financial input, know the business and industry very well!
You may need to syndicate the funds from creditors and lenders such as banks to buy out companies. It all depends on you strategic vision.

But do get good accounting, financial experts and a good lawyer to study the deal. Definitely when you come on stream to take over, your management will discover despite your earlier due diligence, some unpleasant surprises will come out of the woods. Be prepared for this.

But if your mind is made up of the overriding advantage of taking over, then you will ultimately work things out ultimately. You need firmness, focus and extreme courage. It is not for everybody. But it can make huge things happens financially within a short time frame.

5
Technology for Business

Today, the evolving technology would have a direct impact in your business and its outcome.
Humanity will always work much better with technology. Mediocre results can only be gotten if either disregards the other! Neither can replace the other.

The human race for the first time is being connected more than any other donkey years in the past. Many things will never be the same again. *"Things will fall apart"*, quoting late *Prof. Chinua Achebe.*
In the same breath the broken pieces will be realigned and put together for a new shape of things in the affairs of our humanity.

What is the change agent if you ask me?
I.C.T - information, communications and technologies. A drastic change in commerce and industries could be influenced as a result of the so-called "disruptive technology". We are talking about new but useful innovative ideas. These new tools would improve on the scheme of things, both for the consumer and the producer.
The existing way of doing things suddenly are done away with, they become less prominent.
Are you prepared?
Quickly, let us look at the example of, the webinar, for dissemination of information. In the educational industry, technology continues to question the traditional, physical classroom. Knowledge can now be self-served whenever you want it, in the comfort of your space.
That is, I could choose to stream a lecture right across, even to your

handheld phone, anywhere you are located. You do not have to be in my physical presence, to travel around the world to pass that needed information to you. Many examples of such are abounding.

It is all about new ideas, tools or technologies that have changed for the better, the way business is done in many ramifications. New tools which change the old ways - within a short period of time. Yet it doesn't stop there. Technology that optimizes the resources, utilized by a producer, while altering the margins in a business.

Technology that makes product and services, more affordable to consumers. This throws up a level playing field, to many business players across the world. It changes the rules of the game and engagement. Because of ICT - business dogma or paradigm keeps on evolving, with varied experiences.

Tools of the trade are becoming more available and affordable. This has sparked off the entrepreneurial confidence of micro-business owners, who can now make money from their specialized knowledge.
A business made up of one man, could give some bigger companies, a run for their money.
It is an exciting time for Man to excel coupled with the inherent fallout of problems. And many have shared their knowledge with the rest of humanity. It is now about what you can do and less about brandishing, the paper academic qualification you have acquired. Truly so the latter could give you a good starting point.

Now may I warn, technology may not take away all the traditional or classical activities of Man.
I am waiting to see a non-human wine taster that can rival the complex taste buds of a living human-being. This may not become a reality, after all the computer has not entirely erased, the prints or paper from our existence. That's a

consolation of sorts. *A robot yet, cannot be the best idea of baby-seating an infant or teaching good parental values.* Therefore, as I would submit; nothing is absolute but all experiences of Man are just relative.

But technology must be celebrated and capitalized upon. And which human being will not gravitate towards that? The inventions of Man that alleviate problems and equally bring relief. Ignoring technology by a conservative business owner is a recipe for eventual failure.
While at that, you must still be picky, within the avalanche of various shades of tools, churned out daily. A business will not need all applications they are confronted with. Some are simply, a waste of time and resources. In business, one of the goals is to optimize inputs that would give the most rewarding output.

The new mantra you should abide with as a business owner; is to continually ask this very important question, *"what if...?"* It is my personal philosophy I use to prepare for the unexpected.

Technology And Vigilance
The advent of technology forces smart businesses to be on eternal vigilance, against disruption on processes and factors of production.
Let us look at labour. Today, the work-force system is rapidly changing in its coloration. Jobs have been lost and jobs have been created by the advent of the Internet and technology.

The virtual world makes employees recruitment much easier, depending on the type of business. There are affordable professionals that cut across different disciplines that one could source at one's finger tips. This recruitment exercise will demand a different approach of engagement.

You only need to find the right persons that will do your job; to carry out some assignments within your budget. And they are spread across the world.

°MUYIWA OSIFUYE

Such outsourced tasks - as I would love to call them - could be found through the web; just google them. Popular websites will include: *O'desk, Freelancers, Upwork, Fiverr, Craigslist* and many others.

Beside this agglomeration of professionals, we also have employees working on full time, part time or remotely. They come to the physical office only when necessary. But note that there are many businesses, which can only function through physical presence. The factory floor workers will still be at the factory.

Whichever option you choose to engage virtual assistants or experts, you must equally interview them to ensure you get a good bargain, for quality service. Some of these providers may not necessarily be individuals.
A provider may put together a team to attend to your project.
Apply all the precautions as applied in the traditional recruitment; almost all will still come in handy.

Virtual social engagements are evolving and we don't know in which direction is the next frontier. We should be strategic and make the best use of the platforms that meet our entrepreneurial goals.

Imagine the ubiquitous social channels in our lives. Today we hear of *Facebook, Twitter, Instagram, LinkedIn, YouTube, Skype,* lately *WhatsApp* and many others. You don't have to be in all of all of them. Have your business strategy in place to make the right choice.

There are also various blogging platforms, e-commerce platforms and customized applications for highly targeted consumers. They are the new waves of global trends, used for good and not so-good.

Outside of business; localized terrorism, failed ideologies, new ideologies and factions of faith and new knowledge, all push forth their convictions to our face. They create new types of seduced consumers. It is a very dynamic but complicated world but very interesting and could be scary too.

Traditionally speaking, there are many businesses that have become moribund, because they ignored the changing influence of technology and its acceptance by the market.
Sadly, the poster child, as an example is the giant company, Kodak, with its firm erstwhile control of films for cameras. The company downplayed the incursion of the digital camera, into the world of image making.
It was not necessarily due to lack of funds, to diversify into that market and take leadership. It appeared they doubted the technology and possibly wondered if consumer behaviour would welcome that line.

They initially made weak attempts to manufacture digital cameras, but without much conviction they took no further step to do much more. Gradually other manufactures came in; they innovated and found millions of consumers actual accepting the new technology.
The professional photographers that initially stuck to film are presently in the minority. This dwindling and tiny population cannot feed the sales for Kodak, to continue in film production.
(As a professional photographer myself - amongst my other endeavours - I still nurture to shoot on film for personal projects on a few occasions)

The lesson is that the virtual world is sharing strength and relevance, with the real world, almost on equal proportion. A business must embrace the two sides of the divide to enjoy the benefits of both worlds.

Filtering Information Overload

An entrepreneur needs to create time on a regular basis, to read about the industry and related business environment. While there is a need for continuous information, there is a need to be circumspect.
There is so much free information, one could only navigate through the

overload and selectively pick only the relevant nuggets.

Having being infused with this heavy information, you will have to debrief yourself regularly. You have to sieve through all the information you have garnered. Write down the keywords or phrase, which is a good technique, to conjure up all what you have learnt, as entrepreneurs are busy.
Practice what you have internalized through these keywords, in your business leadership activities. Use them according to your business needs and circumstances.
Every country, every locale and certain circumstances in our daily life, and unique business situation, would be the moderating factors to all information, we come across. A few of my thoughts in this book may not be applicable to all readers, and that is the truth. I force myself to carry out this debriefing exercise, because of time famine. I read across different media, both online and offline, thereafter, I come to a conclusion of how to create a synergy, which I must test in my business development.

Website As Capital Asset
Being present on the World Wide Web is a very important tool notwithstanding being an virtual estate.
The business does not have to be Internet based. It is simply another additional platform - with its own peculiarities - to do business, like your physical location.
A website could also be used as an additional tool, to support an offline business, in terms of dissemination of information.
After-all, legislators are yet to leave the hallowed chambers, to debate on the web, but they can be seen to do so, through a web address, real time, in some places.
Technology has removed the need of a formal location for some

businesses. A flourishing business could reside on that small gadget, clasped around in your hands. It could be the smart phone, tablet or laptop connected to the Internet. For some businesses, this has reduced the barrier of high start-up capital.

The simplest of websites can be freely hosted by some online providers. You could have the basic 5 webpages such as *the index, contact, about page, product or service page and gallery page.*
Above all, do note that, websites don't get known, until they are publicized to the target audience. There are billions of webpages and more do join, on a daily basis. You don't build and wait for your target audience to discover it.

However, note that there are successful companies that have just a single webpage, where the summary of the essential part of their activities are described.
This type of website simply shows the summary of their offerings and contact details. They take it up with prospective customers from there. Of course, at the other extreme, there are businesses that have a very robust website, which will include a sophisticated payment page, for e-commerce.

Websites today, are a cocktail of sorts. You mix your own drink, simple or detailed, as it augurs well for your business strategy.
Therefore, the overall outlook must be subject to a deliberate strategy of the business, at a point in time.
You don't just follow the crowd or get carried away with a fancy website, if it does not meet the company's objective – of a good customer experience. Check out the simplicity of sites like Google and others. It about convenience and immediate values for visitors and customers. There is a Nigerian blogger who makes her millions using the free Google blogging platform - *Blogspot* as I write. But I think for newer entrants to blogging, her monetization model becomes more difficult.

°MUYIWA OSIFUYE

The attractive nature of the Internet is the large population and the spread across the world. It is an opportunity where you can apply a simple business model, to sell to millions and equally make millions in cash, at quickly. Find and discover the pain points that affect a large number of people. Most times it might be a simple need which we tend to overlook.

These days people are generally lazy, they would want to be helped with what they can easily do. It is a waiting market on the web. Just sell at a small fee, a negligible figure in the eyes of the average consumer, but count on the millions who would gladly pay. But you have to earn your visitors and mailing list must be worked on.

There are naughty ideas that could bring in money because people are very busy these days or just loved to be pampered. Seriously, it might be worthwhile to find out if there is a need, to teach people how to stand erect.

Something like:

"15secrets on how to stand erect - ramrod like an American Navy Seal".
I just gave you, a steal of an idea. Add your own slant to it.

You also need technology to ensure you can monetize your idea. You may have to pay a one-time fee, to outsource this specialty to experts. You may create an admixture of both online and offline customer experience. There are business models that can be used to generate income.

However, it should be said again, that some businesses can only operate offline, despite their web presence. They must exist in a physical "brick and mortar" space. Their customers need to feel, touch and taste.
So don't box your mindset into a corner, let your entrepreneurial spirit explore possibilities. Even with the online dating going on, you must still meet in flesh and blood someday, to fine-tune your reality.

Remember technology can seduce you to lose your common sense. I see that today!

A beautiful website is not an excuse for sloppy customer experience and a bad product. The web being a powerful phenomenon, with an almost an infinite reach, is neutral to all vices or applause. It doesn't take much, before information becomes viral, across the globe in minutes.
You had better ensure it is for good and not for bad. With fantastic products and a good business system, an appropriate website could be leveraged to achieve rapid business growth.

The Easy Way To Grow?
Growth hacking: that is what they call it.
This is a very relatively new buzz word, especially in online marketing. A "new" disruptive technique that can be used to grow a business. It allows for far less money spent on adverts, yet would yield a much higher rate on investment.
Several start-ups, with modest beginnings have skyrocketed, in terms of millions of patronage and humongous profits, in a very short time.

Examples would include, *Dropbox, Twitter, Facebook*, and others. As I write this, my Firefox browser has been seducing me into their marketing funnel, to tell my friends about their services.
The underlying trick is to create a viral advertising, through the "world of mouth" but lately it's through the tools of technology that are used. And that's cool.

Simply, if a user likes the experience, with the embedded applications or deliberately planned tactic of sharing, others would come on-board. In no time, the rapidity of awareness is much faster than using the traditional advertising technique. It is easily measurable and monitored

°MUYIWA OSIFUYE

It is simply, a new mindset of finding the cheapest ways of reaching out quickly. My thinking is that it is a scion of the classical word-of-mouth notion - known to Man, since time immemorial. I believe there were no billboards, thousands of years ago and yet information was passed around.

However, these very successful companies – internet based - have started to use online software applications and technological tools. They ensure they provide what their niche market wants. They also use simple psychological nudging, to encourage satisfied first time users, to share their experience with others.
Serving as megaphones for these companies, the early users are compensated in various ways. To achieve the same results, the resources deployed for compensation are found to be far less in cost than the traditional advertising campaign. Reaching more consumers is even much faster.
It simply comes down to these steps:
Ensure your products are top notch, meeting the needs of your target consumers. A sloppy product won't take you far; rather it spreads the bad news faster than anything. You may become extinct, in no time.
By the way, technology is a two edged sword.

Get across to your niche only, as the whole consuming world won't be interested in your offering. Approach your niche in trickles. Encourage early adopters to spread the world, provide the means or creative ways that make this easy for them, a tangible gift or bribe. For example, *Dropbox* gives additional data storage space for your referrals those who sign up with them.

Give your customers platforms to speak or publish their testimonials for prospective customers to see, mostly on that website.
Make arrangements to ensure all consumers are brought back into the

loop, so that they can further share their experiences. The power of community is to convince; the so-called peer pressure.
The herd-instinct is at play here. If many are seen doing it, it is assumed to be right; which may also be wrong. Find a way for your clients to come together with their loved ones, whether in your online or offline business.

Organize events regularly, and get more clients. After encouraging your niche audience to swell up their community, you reach a threshold to catapult or be dumped. This threshold is where the experience is accepted and goes viral and develops a life of its own. Thousands and Millions then join in, on autopilot.

From the information garnered from users, you will adjust your offerings to improve on customer experience, on a regular basis. They will always tell you what they want. The business to a large extent must obey this, though there could be an exception, where your vision is sacrosanct.

Above all, the "growth hacking" technique appears much better than the traditional advertising in that, it is measurable and scalable. Certain tools online and offline must be deployed to take the metrics so that you can modify and tinker appropriately. The exercise is not given to accidental results but deliberate actions that must be measured.

Today there is a budding notion that computer geeks are about replacing the traditional marketing professionals, to grow companies. I believe marketers should go for the codes, modify the traditional truths of marketing and make the best of them for optimization, to do their job.

Finally, consider the following points for this new concept:
Think ahead before you come up with your offering that your niche must like.
How would I start a viral revolution, from a few interested clients?

How would I compensate them to tell others?
How would I bring all of them to share their experiences for others to see?
How would I make the offerings meet up with their desires, going by their comments?
And above all, how to deploy the right tools activities, to measure different parameters on customers' experience and business growth?

This new mindset of growth hacking concept can also be extended to the brick and mortar businesses, based offline.
We can look up these highly endowed companies that grew so fast, within a very short time.
Some grew so fast in less than three months, with millions of users coming on board, with little money spent on advertising at the initial stage. That is the goal.

Growth hacking is a developing concept and like other fresh thoughts - many years into the future - another concept would evolve, using the available innovative tools and social psychological observations.
If you like the idea, get freelancers to manage the campaign for you.

6
Your Daily Activities

Let me start here by saying that, at the onset of your business, it is most likely you will be doing so many tasks yourself. But have at the back of your mind that much effort does not necessarily translate to more rewards for the business over time.

To work smart is to derive a process of getting activities carried out, in the most efficient manner. In fact I will explain how you can build a simple system. Much has been explained earlier on in this book.

It simply means a way of carrying specific tasks to achieve a purpose, in a repeatable manner. So you must identify those inputs that get the work done as you want it.
Let me explain further with a simple exercise.
How much have you sold today? A simple question, that is, right? Good! If all the figures have not been recorded, then that is bad. What do you do?

Establish a system for this, which might look like this:
Get a book or use your spread-sheet application in your computer and simply make daily entries. It means whoever needs an answer to that earlier question, he will simply ask for the daily entries. He will look up for each day and possibly the total amount across a period. You don't have to put all these figures in your head.
Another one...

Let's assume you want to reach new customers. You can design something like this.

Every Tuesday and Thursday, schedule on a document that; between 1pm and 2pm, a list of certain physical visits or online must be made, to reach potential consumers.

You will have a checklist of questions and what must be inferred from feedbacks you receive from such an exercise.

You can then measure on that activity of client prospecting.

Whoever that is given that task, will know of any missing portion of the laid out processes when objectives are not being met. It may even be the fault of you, the business owner.

So this is how a simple system is built to help you. It does take time though, to build one. And it doesn't have to be complicated.

Developing An Effective Routine

This all depends on your business or industry. My advice here is just to open your minds to how most entrepreneurs handle their daily schedules at work and outside of it.

You will on a daily basis produce your products and render service to your clients. You will attend to their feedbacks. You will solve problems that have to do with the task at hand, either as an author or a dentist or musician. You will equally plan your time- as expected of you - to do the work.

You will correspond with other people about your business, through available channels. You will also be thinking on how to solve some monetary issues. How to pay back money owed supplier or creditors? How to pursue debtors, to pay up? There will also be a need to oversee your team.

Some days, you just don't feel like doing anything! There may be work that needs to be done but you just don't feel like. It happens. You are not alone. You feel the blues.

Your working environment may not be as exciting as if you were with some other colleagues. As a starter you tend to be alone.
The need for daily motivation has to be developed from inside of you.

You may go out to attend to some other matters, whether directly due to the business or family affair. You come back to the office, if it is too late, you feel guilty that you have not done much for the day. Yet business hasn't been too good, sadly.

And there are days, you feel good, having achieved - much work done, as spelt out by you. It is important to write out a list of what you must do on a daily basis. Don't over-flog yourself if you can't finish them on a particular day. Just roll over.

But be honest with yourself that you maintain a disciplined your mind. With this mindset, you are still better than someone who doesn't have a list of schedule.
The list should be written in indelible ink and not in pencil which is amenable to constant cleaning.
Like it or not there are days, you feel weak. Other days, you feel sleepy on a daily basis; you will know when to take a nap of 20 minute or less. I am good at that. There is no bionic business owner, especially as you get older in age. Delegate and monitor!

Surprisingly when I arrive in the mornings, in spite of a rest overnight, early morning grogginess will not allow me to work immediately. If I don't have an outside assignment, after a 20 minute morning nap, I tend to get fully charged for the rest of the day.

Thereafter, I will usually start to work, getting stronger; from 2pm towards evening. But I must leave the office for home; otherwise towards late evening in the recent years, I could be very alert to do more serious mental work. What I am saying to you in essence is that you should know to deal with your daily activities, as they augur well for your body and business.

Lastly, once the funds are available, start to build your team gradually to achieve your business goal. You will need outsourcing, full-time staff, or both.

Make use of skilled idle hands around your community. Locate young students in the university who are available to work on a callout basis. They could clean the office; work on your PC, or dropping the flyers, and so on. You get my drift, right?

But monitor everything.

Your business strategy and finances should guide you. That's how to grow the business. You can't do it alone, you will burn out. The only contrary opinion to this, is if you are very much okay with your mediocre state of business. If that makes you happy and it is rewarding, you can be a one-man army. Nothing is wrong with that.

7
Your Success & Mistakes

Successful businesses do not drop from the sky, neither are their founders. Likewise those who failed or have bankrupt enterprises in their hands make part of our human reality.
To a very large extent, when you break down all the entrepreneurial efforts to the true basics, as I have explained in this book, your confidence level ought to have been raised by now because of the true perspectives I have given.
It is sweet and it can also be really bitter. You have to negotiate, to win ultimately!
Be resourceful, work smart, seek useful knowledge - which you must act upon - and pray for manifold blessings with abiding faith, that the heavens must smile on your efforts.

Now, you have a fair idea of how most self-employed evolve in the management of their businesses, right from scratch. And you are now aware of how you ought to get things done.

Success in your enterprise is an opportunity to do more. And when you attain that, do capitalize on that outcome. You must applaud and celebrate yourself. But be cautious of changes in time, cycle and trends. These uncontrollable elements may improve for the better or for the worse.

Do I need to say much about mistakes or failures which some gurus tend to glamorize? We only need to learn from these bad experiences, which might be more excruciating to you than to others. But do not over-

celebrate failures! Do not hope and wish for them. As I had mentioned earlier on in this small-business starters guide, you can manage your crisis, if they come. There will a phase of confusion and loss of confidence. You may feel isolated for a while. A year, two years or even five years before the cobwebs clear out.
Be aware that entrepreneurs elsewhere have experienced similar fate. You will find a route to slip through to a much brighter and more rewarding journey - hard lessons having being learnt.
People close to you may not come to your rescue. *"It is your cup of tea"*, they say in their mind.

But I can tell you, what is inside of you is what will set you free or keep your flame extinguished. That flame and spark you had when you ventured into being a founder or a manager of a business. This is the reality. And they do come.

If you don't experience all the challenges that I have highlighted, good luck to your stars. You are simply favoured, that much I can tell you. But watch the sweetness as it lasts.
It is not for me to ascertain how you will deal with the events of things. But take solace in that you won't be the first in your situation and you will never be; be it success or if found at the fringes of some unwelcome situations. Therefore attend to each experience like others before you.

8
Appraisals & The Score Sheet

There must be a time to reflect, to step back and critically look at your milestones carved out at the beginning. What are you reading from them?

Easier said than done? It is extra work but I didn't have a choice. Years back, unknown to me, I was part of the problem to my business. I had a wrong outlook at certain human affairs. Thankfully, *that is corrected now*. However it is an exercise that is never completed throughout the lifecycle of a business of whatever shape, size and guise.

You must find and implement the real solution, if your ship of enterprise is being steered away from your destination.
Get a third party, consultant or an honest folk with fresh eyes for objective analysis. It may be your business or you are the one responsible for the results you are getting. Good or bad. It may be other factors.

As you set out on a journey or a task, it is natural to define an end point or a milestone. This is important so that we can know those goals that need to be identified for measurement. This mindset also applies to a business as an entity.

You will need to schedule a periodical appraisal of your goals through a checklist you started with. Is it monthly, two times a year or yearly? I will suggest as you start out, it must be monthly for at least three years. These periods are the most crucial for your naïve and infant business. The business is very delicate at this point. A lot of structures are still being propped up and you want to know which works or not. Continuous vigilance is needed.

Another advantage is that, it keeps you busy and focused. If you meet up, it will be exciting and inspiring. Yet watch it; for little and big victories. Therefore, strike out each element on your checklist, as you meet the set goals. That stimulates your senses to do more; to go all out, to achieve your preconceived goals.

When you strive to see what is going on, you can know where to make corrections. If otherwise, you do not meet some monthly objectives, do an appraisal, seek advice from a mentor or a small-business consultant and adjust until you get results.
It is a morale booster which gives that boldness when you surmount and rectify things, if they do go wrong. There are times, I have had to abandon some ideas or activities or put them aside for a while. You may come back later when it is more favourable to attend to them.

Having said all these, do not be discouraged about my seemingly discouraging tone. It is simply to prepare your mind. I am incurable optimist too but I don't take things for granted.
I believe with proper scheming and patience, success would come the way of the vigilant, the resourceful and the man and woman of courage and resilience.

9
Is Your CSR Missing the Target?

After you have started to coast home with relish remember, you may want to give back to the society, within your means.

Not too long ago, a billionaire missed his way, somewhere in California - a true life story that I read recently. A lady at a street corner showed him the right direction, as he had lost his way. She was actually giving out handbills to the public, soliciting for donations to undergo a major surgery outside the U.S.

So she equally gave a handbill to this rich man. She didn't know his status. On getting back home, the man had a look at the handbill. He realized the lady who had earlier helped him, was actually begging for money for surgery. He was touched. He therefore, asked his secretary to call her up and decided to give instead the total amount needed.
This was a one-on-one life changing gift. It is possible the man had a foundation, of which its bureaucracy would have missed such individuals, who are in urgent need on our streets.

What I am driving at, is that, the very wealthy, beyond their foundations, should create other channels of reaching out, in person, to ordinary individuals in our societies. There should be more creativity that goes beyond the traditional philanthropic structure.

Under the corporate social responsibility (CSR) activities of businesses, entrepreneurs must ensure that what they give out percolate to the needy in the society and beyond – depending on their capability.
CSR should take further steps and not just to "fulfil all righteousness".

°MUYIWA OSIFUYE

The act of giving must change. Targets are being missed. Benevolence wasted, in spite of all the noise on corporate social responsibility, especially those given by the wealthy across the world.
I salute them though. But there is pattern that looks like an ego trip, another machinery of recycling grants back to the giver.

Therefore, it behoves on a business, no matter how small, once it has found its rhythm to recognize that the enterprise, has not been existing in a vacuum.
It will be good to earmark an amount – affordable to the enterprise - to help causes and individuals within the neighbourhood and beyond. Philanthropists should be more creative than what we see these days, especially where some serious minded individuals simply need, little seed capital.

This brings to my observation, the no-brainer, where the richest in our world, would give money to organizations through their foundations. Granted, this must be done and they should be applauded for this, but there are small businesses that would turn the whole world around for good, with increase in seed money as direct grants. Too much bureaucracy has killed this noble thought.

If monies can't be given, there could be direct patronage of the applicable services and products of these small businesses, by the very rich and their associated companies. Of course quality products these small-businesses must make available.
The very rich should also - on their own - identify those individuals and start-ups with genuine interest, so that they can work with them.
These individuals are not hidden. They are waiting to be discovered but the societal barriers possibly prevent the rich to meet with them in their humble situation.

Many foundations are simply on ego trip, put up for self-glorification. There are very few exceptions though where altruism is it.

Bill Gates, Warren Buffet, Mark Zuckerberg and others in their ilk definitely do give. I applaud them for that. But my submission is that only a small percentage of these monies reach entrepreneurs.

The bureaucracy in these foundations alienates the ordinary would-be entrepreneurs waiting in the wings, across the world, even with their own countries. Granted, there is a global challenge of health issues and similar trends, but money in the right hands could minimize health challenges, indirectly. It looks as if these monies are indirectly being given back to the pharmaceutical companies and the like, where some of these philanthropists are stakeholders. *Maybe...*

A man with money in his pocket is most likely to be a healthier person than an impoverished creative mind. The worthy causes of health, environmental issues should queue behind the need to support the individual-entrepreneurs.
An additional platform different from the Angel investors' financial scheme, as it were, should be established. These monies can come in form of seed capital or as working capital to stabilize a business with a teething problem.
These grants are not simply to discourage creativity, entrepreneurial flair or mental laziness, but to serve as a catalyst for a massive entrepreneurial movement, across the world, to reduce inequality.

It is not about throwing unlimited funds at any start-up. But the capital that gets to small and medium scale businesses are simply much less than what gets to non-profit organizations.

For instance, another way of reducing global illiteracy…
Why not directly help an individual that wants to start an educational

institution or a small school? If you can afford to give out 10,000 units of your currency through your foundation, why not appropriate it this way. Take 8,000 out of this, regarding it as a lottery money, sieve through the news media for that chap, around your neighbourhood or wherever, in need of seed capital.

Ask your assistants to do a background check on the person, to understand his commitment and passion of his entrepreneurial dream. They may even be a group.

It does not disrupt your foundation or your Angel investing business. This is a person to person model. This gift could be for such businesses to take off. Maybe the young founder has a non-terminal health problem or his legal fees is militating against his freedom, pushing the business towards extinction? The remainder 2,000 could go for other developmental or health issues elsewhere.

Earlier on I had advised why it is safe for entrepreneurs to be frugal and to keep money aside. But one needs to be realistic, as some crisis in business or personal life, not due to our own making, may prevent us from saving. Events do happen, that make it impossible to spare a single cent, to even keep that aside.

Such people who are in dire need, either due to high health bills, starvation, homelessness or other unwelcome harsh realities of the world; they simply cannot save! Because there is no physical cash with them, the only hope is to be inspired with wisdom, to bring something of value to the market place.

This can then be exchanged for pecuniary rewards. They can build up from here. But some smart ideas and execution can't do without seed capital.

It is true that some are not so lucky or endowed, or depression has taken a toll. It is not because they are lazy. When such business owners approach a foundation to seek for a way out, we must hear them out first.

Ask them what they really want before you thrust into their laps an incongruous form to fill *"of possible assistance"* and schedule of terms of what you desire to sponsor. Should it be about you or others if you really know the pains out there, where the greatest amount of needs is situated?

If your business can't afford what they desire, do your own little. Rally your well-to-do contemporaries, to render collective assistance, to lift others up. The joy so derived, can't be measured, eternally. After-all, you claim you can do without the money as a non-profit gesture.

10
What Is Next?

Let's assume you have now gotten used to the rhythm of managing a business as a self-employed or as a founder; possibly some of your goals have been met within the time frame you set out. This could be three years or more. One thing you must not forget is that; do realize that your business must have gotten to a phase where it should run, on its own in your absence.

That is, the operational procedures must have been put in place. This is where a competent and honest team, apart from you could oversee the business in your absence, if you wish.
This may not apply to all businesses. But that is one of the goals of entrepreneurship.

If you have not achieved this very sensitive stage, you are simply a growing business or an employee working in your business. You simply did not work on your business as an entity, which should have developed its own culture, personality and goals.
Why am I saying this? Do not let the pains of being a founder suck you away from using the resources available to you, that you can afford to create an independent organization. I am referring to the abounding human and material resources that should make the business to run profitably.

Once you achieve this goal with the proper mindset, you never can tell other opportunities may come your way. These would include the need to explore elsewhere, to make more money or do something…non-profit, if that augurs well with your soul.

You may wish to take some rest. You may even have an offer by investors who would like to buy this business outright or buy into a portion of your stakes
Your business as a profitable system – can now be likened to a good and well packaged product - resting on a retailer's shelf, waiting for the highest bidder, if you choose to release it.

You may get to this point in less than five years or more. It all depends. So I wish you well into the exciting world of enterprise.

Want Timely Information About My New Books and Free Resources?

- For your new releases, articles, free resources and relevant information visit **www.muyiwaosifuye.com**

- **For coaching and consulting: send me an email:**
  mosifuye@gmail.com
  contact@muyiwaosifuye.com

- **For Business Tips And Insights**
  http://www.twitter.com/rbizchat

- **The Watering Hole: Join Me With Others**
  www.facebook.com/StomRuby

- **Search for** "Muyiwa Osifuye" on **YouTube** to Subscribe to my channel for Tips and further useful information.

- Watch my books on review on Channels TV, (a topmost TV station in Nigeria) here:
  https://youtu.be/DjAWf4ckeAs

About The Author

'MUYIWA OSIFUYE was born in Lagos, in January 1960.
He has a degree in Optometry (1984) from the University of Benin, Nigeria.
He has an MBA – specialising in Marketing & Finance (1991) from the University of Lagos, Nigeria and also a Diploma (2002) in Professional Photography from the New York Institute of Photography, USA.
He lives in Lagos, Nigeria

I hope you have enjoyed this guide.
It will be kind of you to do me a "small favour".
Could you please write a few words to review this book on Amazon.
Your thoughts would guide me to write more books and articles that would be beneficial to you and others.

www.ingramcontent.com/pod-product-compliance
Lightning Source LLC
Chambersburg PA
CBHW070252190526
45169CB00001B/380